New Trends on Human–Computer Interaction

José A. Macías · Toni Granollers ·
Pedro Latorre Andrés

Editors

New Trends
on Human–Computer
Interaction

Research, Development, New Tools
and Methods

Foreword by Angel Puerta

 Springer

Editors

José A. Macías
Escuela Politécnica Superior
Depto. Ingeniería Informática
Universidad Autonoma de Madrid
Avda. Tomás y Valiente, 11
28049 Madrid
Spain
j.macias@uam.es

Toni Granollers
Depto. Informàtica i
Enginyeria Industrial
Universitat Lleida
c/de Jaume II, 69
25001 Lerida
Campus Cappon
Spain
tonig@diei.udl.cat

Pedro Latorre Andrés
Depto. Informática e
Ingeniería de Sistemas
Universidad Zaragoza
María de Luna, 1
50018 Zaragoza
Spain
platorre@unizar.es

ISBN 978-1-84996-839-3   e-ISBN 978-1-84882-352-5
DOI 10.1007/978-1-84882-352-5

Springer Science+Business Media
springer.com

Preface

This book comprises a variety of breakthroughs and recent advances on Human–Computer Interaction (HCI) intended for both researchers and practitioners. Topics addressed here can be of interest for those people searching for last trends involving such a growing discipline. Important issues concerning this book includes cutting-edge topics such as Semantic Web Interfaces, Natural Language Processing and Mobile Interaction, as well as new methodological trends such as Interface-Engineering techniques, User-Centred Design, Usability, Accessibility, Development Methodologies and Emotional User Interfaces. The idea behind this book is to bring together relevant and novel research on diverse interaction paradigms. New trends are guaranteed according to the demanding claims of both HCI researchers and practitioners, which encourage the explicit arrangement of new industrial and technological topics such as the previously cited Interfaces for the Semantic Web, and Mobile Interfaces, but also Multimodal Interaction, Collaborative Interfaces, End-User Development, Usability and User Interface Engineering.

Chapters included in this book comprise a selection of top high-quality papers from Interacción 2007, which is the most important HCI conference sponsored by AIPO (the Spanish HCI Association). Papers were selected from a ranking obtained through double-blind peer review and later meta-review processes, considering the best evaluated paper from both the review and presentation session. Such a paper selection constitutes only 33% of the papers published in the conference proceedings.

We would like to thank the reviewers for their effort in revising the chapters included in this publication, namely Silvia T. Acuña, Sandra Baldasarri, Crescencio Bravo, Cesar A. Collazos, Antonio Díaz, Xavier Ferré, Nestor Garay, Francisco García, Roberto García, José L. Garrido, Miguel Gea, Rosa Gil, José M. González, María P. González, Toni Granollers, Francisco L. Gutiérrez, Pedro Latorre, María D. Lozano, José A. Macías, Mari Carmen Marcos, Mario A. Moreno, Roberto Moriyón, Raquel Navarro, Manuel Ortega, Oscar Pastor, Miguel A. Redondo, Arcadio Reyes and Gustavo Rossi.

José A. Macías
Toni Granollers
Pedro Latorre Andrés

Foreword

In its classical role, a scientific congress is a vehicle to understand and analyze the latest advances, discoveries, and findings in a field. Through the chapters in this book, readers will have ample opportunity to explore some of the best contributions presented at Interacción 2007, the annual meeting of the human–computer interaction community in Spain. A vast number of subfields are represented in this book including computer-supported collaborative work, user-centered design, user interface tools, and virtual reality among others.

Beyond its classical sense, however, an annual scientific congress such as Interacción is the perfect vehicle to take the pulse of a scientific community. What are the most active research areas, what is the nature of the research itself, who drives the work, industry or academia, and how the community compares to others around the world are some of the interesting questions that an analysis of a conference results can answer. Let us therefore examine briefly what are the trends that Interacción 2007 reveals.

First, we notice the remarkably empirical essence of most of the work. By nature and by its youth as a discipline, human–computer interaction tends to favor empirical over theoretical work. But the tendency here is much stronger. Research projects are clearly directed at applying innovations and testing hypotheses via practical cases. We see more mainstream situations such as collaborative techniques to support education and learning. Notwithstanding the abundance of empirical efforts, there is as well a clear presence for research of a more formal bent especially in the areas of model-based interface development, and user interface specification languages. Overall, we get a picture of a community that emphasizes practical results and in doing so presents a contrast to the work in several other fields in computer science, which most notably in Europe tend to favor formal methods.

Second, we observe a trend to an abundant amount of work in the areas of usability and evaluation. Projects range from the characterization for usability of collaborative environments to the definition of accessibility concerns for users with special needs. In highlighting usability, Interacción 2007 does conform to recent developments seen in many other user interface conferences. As the field matures, the number of discoveries and inventions of a highly novel nature decreases. This is a natural evolution that takes the field toward advances of an incremental, as opposed to revolutionary character. Progress becomes more measurable, comparative evaluations are needed in order to show improvements, and users take precedence over systems and techniques. In general, this trend is a mixed bag. On one hand, usability is the ultimate goal of user-interface design efforts and clearly there is little value in creating new, but unusable systems. On the other hand, readers of recent human–computer interaction papers will yearn somewhat for the early days of the field when seemingly each paper presented a brand-new idea.

Third, we see a clear favoritism toward exploring the engineering aspects of user interfaces as opposed to the psychological factors of said interfaces. We find tools to manipulate languages and patterns, virtual reality environments for medical applications, and various methodologies for the design and development of interfaces. It is clear that over the years a certain unease in the field has developed between those who see human–computer interaction as mainly a human activity and those who see it as a system where the human participates. Each perspective leads to significantly different research philosophies and consequently to substantially different research efforts. Large conferences, such as CHI, the annual meeting of the human–computer interaction group of the Association for Computing Machinery, struggle with this issue and end up unsuccessfully trying to accommodate all factions under one roof. For the time being at least, Interacción does not suffer from this malady and presents a cohesive front as to the overall philosophy and direction of the research.

Finally, we notice a healthy dose of cooperation, and technology transition, among academia, industry, and government. This aspect is obviously facilitated by the empirical emphasis of the work, which was noted above. Needless to say, such cooperation is far from ideal and where we to ask the actors in each project about this topic we would surely find them wanting much more. However, avenues seem to be open for government to support work and for academia to transition results to industry. It will be definitely interesting in future years to observe whether this appearance of cooperation evolves into a solid framework.

In sum, we present in this book what should be an exciting mix of ideas, proposals, methods, artifacts, and results. An exploration into the philosophy, trends, and concerns of the human–computer interaction community in Spain. A compendium of who is who and what is happening where. And, an archive of reference for future work. May you the reader enjoy!

Redwhale Software, CA USA   Angel Puerta

Contents

Contributors

David Anaya Advanced Computer Graphics Group (GIGA), Aragon Institute for Engineering Research (I3A), University of Zaragoza, Zaragoza, Spain.

Pedro Latorre Andrés Dept. de Information Systems and Engineering, Centro Politécnico Superior, Universidad de Zaragoza, Zaragoza, Spain, platorre@unizar.es

Nathalie Aquino Centro de Investigación en Métodos de Producción de Software, Universidad Politécnica de Valencia, Camino de Vera S/N, Valencia, Spain, naquino@pros.upv.es

Sandra Baldassarri Advanced Computer Graphics Group (GIGA), Aragon Institute for Engineering Research (I3A), University of Zaragoza, Zaragoza, Spain, sandra@unizar.es

M.J. Cabrera Videogames and E-Learning Research Lab. (LIVE) – GEDES. Software Engineering Department, University of Granada, C/ Daniel Saucedo Aranda s/n, Granada, Spain, mcabrera@ugr.es

Valentín Cardeñoso-Payo ECA-SIMM Laboratory, Universidad de Valladolid. Campus Miguel Delibes s/n, Valladolid, Spain, valen@infor.uva.es

Anna Carreras Institut Universitari de l'Audiovisual, Universitat Pompeu Fabra, Tànger, Barcelona, Spain, acarreras@iua.upf.edu

Eva Cerezo Advanced Computer Graphics Group (GIGA), Aragon Institute for Engineering Research (I3A), University of Zaragoza, Zaragoza, Spain.

Cesar A. Collazos IDIS Research Group, University of Cauca, Popayan, Colombia, ccollazo@unicauca.edu.co

David Escudero-Mancebo ECA-SIMM Laboratory, Universidad de Valladolid, Campus Miguel Delibes s/n, Valladolid, Spain, descuder@infor.uva.es

Isabel Fernández-Castro Department of Computer Languages and Systems, University of the Basque Country U.P.V./E.H.U., Spain, isabel.fernandez@ehu.es

José A. Gallud Computer Systems Department, University of Castilla-La Mancha, Albacete, Spain, jose.gallud@uclm.es

Arturo S. García Laboratory of User Interaction and Software Engineering (LoUISE), Instituto de Investigación en Informática de Albacete (I3A), Universidad de Castilla-La Mancha, Campus universitario s/n, Albacete, Spain, arturo@dsi.uclm.es

Roberto García Universitat de Lleida, Jaume II 69, Lleida, Spain, rgarcia@diei.udl.cat

José Luis Garrido Dpto. de Lenguajes y Sistemas Informáticos, Universidad de Granada, E.T.S.I.I.T., C/ Periodista Daniel Saucedo Aranda, s/n, Granada, Spain, jgarrido@ugr.es

Rosa Gil Universitat de Lleida, Jaume II 69, Lleida, Spain, rgil@diei.udl.cat

William J. Giraldo Systems and Computer Engineering, University of Quindío, Quindío, Colombia, wjgiraldo@uniquindio.edu.co

Arturo González-Escribano ECA-SIMM Laboratory, Universidad de Valladolid. Campus Miguel Delibes s/n, Valladolid, Spain, arturo@infor.uva.es

César González-Ferreras ECA-SIMM Laboratory, Universidad de Valladolid. Campus Miguel Delibes s/n, Valladolid, Spain, cesargf@infor.uva.es

Gabriel González Laboratory of User Interaction and Software Engineering (LoUISE), Instituto de Investigación en Informática de Albacete (I3A), Universidad de Castilla-La Mancha, Campus universitario s/n, Albacete, Spain.

J.L. González Sánchez Videogames and E-Learning Research Lab. (LIVE) – GEDES. Software Engineering Department. University of Granada, C/ Daniel Saucedo Aranda, s/n, Granada, Spain, joseluis@ugr.es

Pascual González Laboratory of User Interaction and Software Engineering (LoUISE), Instituto de Investigación en Informática de Albacete (I3A), Universidad de Castilla-La Mancha, Campus universitario s/n, Albacete, Spain, pgonzalez@dsi.uclm.es

Toni Granollers Department of Languages and Informatics Systems, University of Lleida, Lleida, Spain, tonig@diei.udl.cat

F.L. Gutiérrez Videogames and E-Learning Research Lab. (LIVE) – GEDES. Software Engineering Department, University of Granada, C/ Daniel Saucedo Aranda, s/n, Granada, Spain, fgutierr@ugr.es

Miguel J. Hornos Dpto. de Lenguajes y Sistemas Informáticos, Universidad de Granada, E.T.S.I.I.T., C/ Periodista Daniel Saucedo Aranda, s/n, Granada, Spain, mhornos@ugr.es

María Visitación Hurtado Dpto. de Lenguajes y Sistemas Informáticos, Universidad de Granada, E.T.S.I.I.T., C/ Periodista Daniel Saucedo Aranda, s/n, Granada, Spain, mhurtado@ugr.es

Elena Lafuente Lapena Laboratorio Aragones de Usabilidad. Parque Tecnológico Walqa Ed.1. Cuarte, Huesca, Spain, elafuente@laboratoriousabilidad.com

Begoña Losada Department of Computer Languages and Systems, University of the Basque Country U.P.V./E.H.U., Spain, b.losada@ehu.es

Maria D. Lozano Computer Systems Department, University of Castilla-La Mancha, Albacete, Spain, maria.lozano@uclm.es

José A. Macías Universidad Autónoma de Madrid, Tomás y Valiente 11, Madrid, Spain, j.macias@uam.es

Diego Martínez Laboratory of User Interaction and Software Engineering (LoUISE), Instituto de Investigación en Informática de Albacete (I3A), Universidad de Castilla-La Mancha, Campus universitario s/n, Albacete, Spain, diegomp1982@dsi.uclm.es

Ana I. Molina Laboratorio CHICO. Escuela Superior de Informática. Universidad de Castilla-La Mancha, Paseo de la Universidad 4, Ciudad Real, Spain, AnaIsabel.Molina@uclm.es

José P. Molina Laboratory of User Interaction and Software Engineering (LoUISE), Instituto de Investigación en Informática de Albacete (I3A), Universidad de Castilla-La Mancha, Campus universitario s/n, Albacete, Spain, jpmolina@dsi.uclm.es

Manuel Noguera Dpto. de Lenguajes y Sistemas Informáticos, Universidad de Granada, E.T.S.I.I.T., C/ Periodista Daniel Saucedo Aranda, s/n, Granada, Spain, mnoguera@ugr.es

Marta Oliva Universitat de Lleida. Jaume II 69, Lleida, Spain, oliva@diei.udl.cat

Héctor Olmedo-Rodríguez ECA-SIMM Laboratory, Universidad de Valladolid. Campus Miguel Delibes s/n, Valladolid, Spain, holmedo@infor.uva.es

Manuel Ortega Department of Technologies and Information Systems, University of Castilla – La Mancha, Ciudad Real, Spain, Manuel.Ortega@uclm.es

P. Paderewski Videogames and E-Learning Research Lab. (LIVE) – GEDES. Software Engineering Department, University of Granada, C/ Daniel Saucedo Aranda, s/n, Granada, Spain, patricia@ugr.es

Ignacio Panach Centro de Investigación en Métodos de Producción de Software, Universidad Politécnica de Valencia, Camino de Vera S/N, Valencia, Spain, jpanach@pros.upv.es

Narcís Parés Institut Universitari de l'Audiovisual, Universitat Pompeu Fabra, Tànger, Barcelona, Spain, npares@iua.upf.edu

Oscar Pastor Centro de Investigación en Métodos de Producción de Software, Universidad Politécnica de Valencia, Camino de Vera s/n, Valencia, Spain, opastor@pros.upv.es

Victor M.R. Penichet Computer Systems Department, University of Castilla-La Mancha, Albacete, Spain, victor.penichet@uclm.es

Ferran Perdrix Diari Segre. Del Riu 6, Lleida, Spain; Universitat de Lleida. Jaume II 69, Lleida, Spain, fperdrix@diarisegre.com

Matthieu Poyade Departamento de Tecnología Electrónica, ETSI de Telecomunicación, Universidad de Málaga, Spain, matthieu.poyade@uma.es

Miguel A. Redondo Laboratorio CHICO. Escuela Superior de Informática. Universidad de Castilla-La Mancha, Paseo de la Universidad 4, Ciudad Real, Spain, Miguel.Redondo@uclm.es

Arcadio Reyes-Lecuona Departamento de Tecnología Electrónica, ETSI de Telecomunicación, Universidad de Málaga, Spain, areyes@uma.es

María Luisa Rodríguez Dpto. de Lenguajes y Sistemas Informáticos, Universidad de Granada, E.T.S.I.I.T., C/ Periodista Daniel Saucedo Aranda, s/n, Granada, Spain, mlra@ugr.es

Francisco Royo-Santas Advanced Computer Graphics Group (GIGA), Aragon Institute for Engineering Research (I3A), University of Zaragoza, Zaragoza, Spain.

Ricardo Tesoriero Computer Systems Department, University of Castilla-La Mancha, Albacete, Spain, ricardo@dsi.uclm.es

Luis Mena Tobar Laboratorio Aragones de Usabilidad. Parque Tecnológico Walqa Ed.1. Cuarte, Huesca, Spain. luis@menasl.com

Maite Urretavizcaya Department of Computer Languages and Systems, University of the Basque Country U.P.V./E.H.U., Spain, maite.urretavizcaya@ehu.es

Francisco Valverde Centro de Investigación en Métodos de Producción de Software, Universidad Politécnica de Valencia, Camino de Vera s/n, Valencia, Spain, fvalverde@pros.upv.es

Raquel Viciana-Abad Departamento de Ingeniería de Telecomunicación, EPS Linares, Universidad de Jaén, Spain, rviciana@ujaen.es

N. Padilla Zea Videogames and E-Learning Research Lab. (LIVE) – GEDES. Software Engineering Department, University of Granada, C/ Daniel Saucedo Aranda, s/n, Granada, Spain, npadilla@ugr.es

Chapter 1
An Automatic Rule-Based Translation System to Spanish Sign Language (LSE)

Sandra Baldassarri and Francisco Royo-Santas

Abstract   This chapter presents an automatic translation system from Spanish language into Spanish Sign Language (LSE) based on the use of grammar and morphology rules in order to ensure its versatility. The system accepts input from spoken or written Spanish and the output corresponds to a representation format adaptable and interpretable by any other system capable of producing animations. The translation of a sentence or phrase is carried out in four steps, each of which is performed by a different module: a morphosyntactic analyzer, a grammatical transformer, a morphological transformer and, finally, a sign generator. The system has been successfully integrated in a 3D animation engine and has been tested with a series of phrases, with very satisfactory results, both in speed and in quality.

1.1 Introduction

In the last few years, the design of computer application interfaces has evolved in order to improve efficiency, effectiveness, and user satisfaction by way of the usability engineering approach. Nowadays, the design of a device or program without taking the final users and their capacities into account would be strictly devoid of sense. Universal design tries to guarantee the accessibility of applications and technologies, regardless of whether users are affected by disabilities or not.

One group of users that has been closely studied by this discipline is the deaf community. Although at first sight the transformation of information into text messages might seem to solve their problems, the reality of the situation is somewhat more complex. Deaf people do not understand Spanish in the same way as people who can hear, especially if they were born deaf. Thus, they have more difficulty reading and writing in Spanish than in their true language, sign language, because

S. Baldassarri (✉)
Advanced Computer Graphics Group (GIGA), Aragon Institute for Engineering Research (13A), University of Zaragoza, Spain
e-mail: sandra@unizar.es

J.A. Macías et al. (eds.), *New Trends on Human–Computer Interaction*,
DOI 10.1007/978-1-84882-352-5_1, © Springer-Verlag London Limited 2009

they do not have mental images of every word or cannot determine the semantics of every word and construction, as is often the case, e.g., with prepositions. This poses, therefore, the need to develop tools that allow translation into sign language. However, we must keep in mind that automatic translation involves additional complications because, contrary to popular belief, this language is not universal: each country has its own variety and some of them, such as Spain, have several.

In order to develop a complete and versatile system, a comprehensive study of Spanish Sign Language was carried out to begin with, using several books [1–3], web pages [4, 5] (amongst others) and interviews with translators in order to compare the construction of Spanish Sign Language (LSE) with Spanish and establish which patterns to use in translations.

Throughout the world there are several projects in this field which are currently attempting to automatically translate or adapt written languages to sign language. ViSiCAST [6–8] and eSIGN [9], two large-scale projects geared towards providing access to information to the deaf population within the European Union, deserve special mention. Considerable effort was invested in these systems in order to develop powerful systems capable of integrating every phase of translation, including visualization by means of an avatar. However, the languages involved in these projects are all far removed from Spanish [10], grammatically very more complex.

In Spain there is also an interesting project in which the translation is based on the creation of rules which allow the extraction of the semantics of words in order to subsequently group them and give rise to signs. Despite the underlying idea is good one and that the project is being developed in Spain, it is also focused on English grammar [8]. Within the Spanish grammar, there is a project that involves from voice analysis to gesture generation [11]. Despite having achieved very good results, the rules used are highly dependent on context and adapt only to a specific problem and its morphological characteristics. There are also several statistical translation based systems [12]. The main drawback of this method is that it is too *general*; it is used for any type of translation and, unlike those which are based on rules, the results of a translation for which it has not been coached can be quite unpredictable.

Considering the LSE studies and the investigation of previous work on automatic translation tools into LSE, we decide to develop a system using "Spanish grammar" as basis. This system performs a series of transformations in which the *syntactical* and *morphological* characteristics of words and also the *semantics* of their meaning are taken into account. In this way, a system adapted to the specific problem of translating Spanish into LSE will be developed. And the use of Spanish grammar and its adaptation to Spanish and LSE are the main novelties of the design. The advantage of our system is that it is based on rules, and therefore, when fed input for which it is not prepared, it will always generate output that is in keeping with the rules of LSE. Another feature which distinguishes our system from previous research is the capacity to modify translations depending on the interpreter's mood. In order to do this, the input of a parameter indicating mood is allowed (e.g., whether the interpreter is happy, angry, etc.) so that translations may vary, just like they do when LSE interpretation is performed by a human being.

1.2 The Automatic Translation System

For the automatic translation from spoken or written Spanish into LSE, our system performs a series of transformations in which the *syntactical* and *morphological* characteristics of words and also the *semantics* of their meaning are taken into account. As can be seen in Fig. 1.1, the translation of a sentence or phrase is carried out in four steps, each of which is performed by a different module.

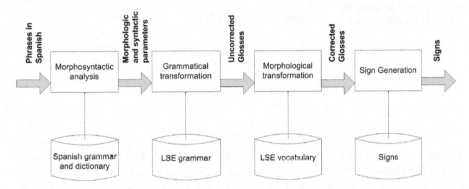

Fig. 1.1   General view of the system

1.2.1 Step 1: Morphosyntactic Analysis

The first step involves both morphological and syntactical analysis of each sentence or phrase in order to obtain the characteristics of the words (root, type, gender, etc.) and the relations of syntactical dependency existing among them. A phrase in Spanish is used as input, and a series of parameters containing all the morphological information of the words as well as the relations and syntactical dependencies among them are drawn from it.

Sentences can be considered as a group of related blocks such as subject, predicate, verb, etc. Each of these blocks, the subject for instance, is in turn comprised of likewise related subblocks, such as a noun phrase, a genitive, etc. Thus, the phrase can be successively subdivided into smaller blocks until we come to the smallest units, words. Each of these blocks has a nucleus comprised of the most important word. Therefore, a relation of dependency between superior and inferior blocks can be represented as a dependency between their respective nuclei. The nucleus of the main phrase shall thus be its most important word, usually the verb.

In order to store the information, we use a dependency tree which allows the representation of relations by means of a tree, the nodes of which are the nucleus words. These nodes store all the morphological information associated to the word and the block it represents (type of block, function within the phrase, etc.). This

representation is based on the dependency analysis performed by the FreeLing application [13]. This software was chosen due to its great versatility, power and, type
of license.

Fig. 1.2 Dependency tree of
the phrase El padre de mi
amigo ha comido un segundo
plato en el comedor ("My
friend's father ate a second
course in the dining room")

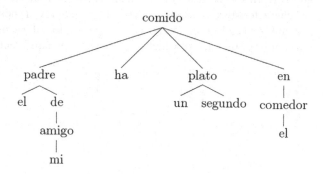

Example. Figure 1.2 shows an example of the dependency tree established by analyzing the phrase *"El padre de mi amigo ha comido un segundo plato en el comedor"*. The most important word in the example is the verb "comido," from which
hang the nuclei of the blocks depending on the verb: "padre" (on *"el padre de mi
amigo"*), "ha" (auxiliary of the verb), "plato" (*"un segundo plato"*), and "en" (on
"en la mesa"). In turn, "el" and "de" hang from "padre" (represented by the genitive
"de mi amigo").

1.2.2 Step 2: Grammatical Transformation

On the basis of the syntactic information gathered during the previous step, and
through the application of a series of grammatical rules, this module generates
a series of glosses (where a gloss is a representation of a sign in the form of a
word) which, although in keeping with grammatical rules, are still not fully correct
in LSE.

Grammatical transformation is carried out in reverse order, using *bottom-up* techniques. Thus, we start from the leaves of the tree and the translation's information
is gradually transmitted to the higher levels. Each new level reached receives all the
information from the nodes hanging from it. According to the type of node (whether
it is a noun phrase, a genitive, a verb group, etc.), there are specific rules associated
to it which determine how to group these words. For instance, a noun phrase is translated by placing the noun first and adjectives and genitives next. There are two types
of information transmitted to one level from the levels subordinated to it: semantic information and the already done translation of that part of the phrase. Semantic information is used to gain extra information regarding the units and aspects
of the phrase. For instance, in a given phrase, both place and time belong to the
same block (noun phrase with a preposition), but they differ only in their semantics.

Semantics includes meaning, temporal, and numeral information, and information regarding the type of block. In order to gather these data, it was necessary to implement a dictionary including several types of information associated to words, such as the meaning they convey (temporal, local, etc.); in many cases, this information is essential for performing a translation, because the order in the final sentence depends on semantic, as temporal information must appear before local information, for instance.

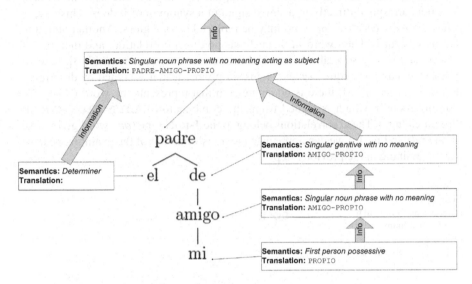

Fig. 1.3 Explanatory graph of the data flow in the block *"el padre de mi amigo"*

Example. Figure 1.3 shows an explanatory graph of information flow for the translation of the *"el padre de mi amigo"* block from the example studied in the previous section. As already mentioned, the process starts with the leaves of the tree. The word *"mi"* is analyzed as a first person possessive and translated as PROPIO. This information is passed on to *"amigo,"* which blends it with its own information as a noun, generating AMIGO-PROPIO and the information typical of a noun phrase. In turn, it is sent to *"de,"* which adds its own and sends it to *"padre."* This word, after gathering the information from all of its offspring, *"el"* and *"de,"* along with the information from the word "padre," sends all the resulting information to the next level, in this case a noun phrase that functions as the subject and which is translated as PADRE-AMIGO-PROPIO. The final information received by the root will lead to the final translation of the entire phrase, which in this case would be: COMEDOR-PADRE--AMIGO-PROPIO-SEGUNDO-PLATO-COMER.

1.2.3 Step 3: Morphological Transformation

Although the sentence produced in the previous step is in keeping with the grammatical rules of LSE, the glosses which make it up are not correct, because they do not translate directly into signs, since they do not comply with LSE's morphological rules. The necessary changes for direct translation into signs are implemented in this part of the translation process. Failure to comply with LSE's morphological rules can be due to several reasons: The simplest case is when the word in Spanish does not correspond directly to a single sign but a synonym of it does. This case is called **1-to-1's**, because *one* word may be replaced by *one* gloss. Another situation that may occur is that a word in Spanish has no direct correlation, and therefore it is necessary to sign several words, which is the case of hyperonyms [2, 3]. A word in Spanish may also require several signs simply because it is signed by describing it. For instance, in LSE there is no single sign that represents the word COMEDOR ("dining room"), which is signed using the combination HABITACIÓN-COMER ("room-eating"). These correlations belong to the **1-to-N** type (*one* word giving rise to *several*). In Fig. 1.4 we can appreciate the transformation of the example we have been examining in the previous step.

Fig. 1.4 1-to-N transformation in which COMEDOR (dining room) becomes HABITACIÓN-COMER (room + eating)

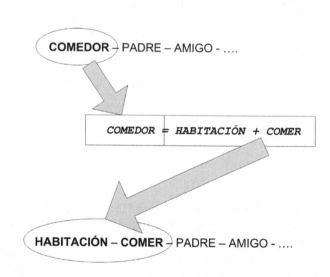

The opposite case is also possible, i.e., the representation of several words in Spanish by a single sign in LSE. This problem turns up mostly in expressions made up of several words, such as TENER-RAZÓN (*tener la razón*) or DAR-BESO (*dar un beso*), which are signed with a single sign.[1] These transformations are called **N-a-1**, since *several* words become a *single* gloss. Figure 1.5 shows an example of this case.

---

[1] Respectively and literally in the second case, "To be right" and "to give a kiss" (translator's note).

Fig. 1.5 N-to-1
transformation in which
DAR (give) and BESO (kiss)
become BESAR (to kiss)

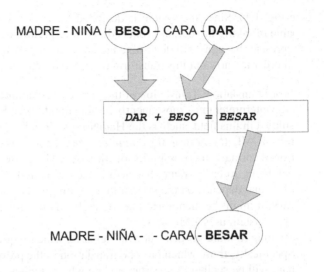

In order to implement these transformations, we decided to design a dictionary containing all these equivalences on the A=B form, in which A represents the word sequence which has to be found in the original phrase and B the words which have to be replaced.

The methodology followed to implement these transformations requires running over the sentence and carrying out substitutions for each of the words. The algorithm applied to each of these sentences involves the dictionary supplying every possible transformation beginning with that word. This will determine the substitution percentage for each of these, i.e., how many of the words that make it up are present in the original phrase. This review of possible substitutions begins with those phrases that contain the largest number of words and ends with single-word ones; this ensures that should there be several possible substitutions, the one that contains more words will always be implemented.

When a percentage of 100% is reached, i.e., when all the words on the left side of the equivalence (A) have been located, these are deleted from the original phrase, with the exception of the first one, which will be replaced by all the relevant words from part B. The effect can be seen in Fig. 1.5, in which BESO disappears once the two words due for substitution (DAR and BESO) have been located. As a result of this process, after running through the entire sentence, we end up with a succession of glosses which are both correct and directly *signable*.

1.2.4 Step 4: Sign Generation

Once the appropriate glosses have been produced (those which correspond directly to signs), in this step they are translated into a representation format that allows the system responsible for interpreting the results to generate the relevant animations (see Fig. 1.1). Since the system is designed for integration within a larger system capable of taking the output produced and interpreting it, the final method chosen to represent the signs will determine the animation system.

In order to carry out this transformation, the module is divided into three parts:

1. Word translation: Translation of the glosses into an intermediate format that the sign interpreter must subsequently be able to interpret. Several formats have been studied in this field, such as the HamNoSys (*Hamburg Notation System*) [14] or the SiGML (*Signing gesture markup language*). Besides the previously mentioned formats, the possibility of direct translation to script orders in formats belonging to each system has also been considered. However, the final choice of format depends on the system that is going to perform the animation. In any case, it might be mentioned that versatility is maximum, since the fully developed system uses XML files.
2. Spelling module: In LSE there are glosses which require dactylogical *spelling*. Specifically, those which have no translation in the previously mentioned dictionary will be spelled. A specific module which divides words into letters according to the characteristics of Spanish, such as the groupings RR, CH, or LL, which have their own signs in LSE, is created for this purpose.
3. Other signs: There are other important elements besides words which are directly translatable to signs, such as the translator's mood swings or gestures related to expression. These "special signs" require special translation, although this is compatible with the word dictionary. In order to represent this information, a series of special glosses enclosed within "<>" are created. These contain explicit orders, such as "emphasize with a look" or "look upset".

1.3 Inclusion of Mood

The mood of a deaf person influences the way that the person will communicate, just like anyone else. In this case, the construction of phrases and the signs that make them up are modified on the one hand, and the final realization of the signs is modified on the other.

In the fully developed system, the inclusion of mood provokes changes in two translation phases: grammatical rules are modified, and so is the final transformation of the signs.

1. **Grammatical transformation:** As we have seen, each type of block is associated to a series of rules pertaining to its form and function. These procedures are modified to change the way of generating the translations according to mood swings. Mood influences meaning and leads to the repetition of certain words, such as the nucleus, or to the appearance of new ones (similar to question tags or pet expressions). However, it can also be the case that certain blocks alter the order of the words within them to emphasize some of them.

2. **Sign generation:** Mood also influences the way in which specific words are signed. Thus, e.g., the word "no" can be accompanied by different gestures. When the person signing is happy, he or she will move their finger, but if the person is angry, he or she usually resorts to dactylology and signs "N–O". In order to take these cases into account, the dictionary used for final translation of the glosses into the chosen language of representation has been modified, allowing one and the same word to be translated differently depending on the mood parameter.

1.4 Results

1.4.1 Feature Measurements

The quality of translations was tested, by means of a presentation composed of 92 sentences, with 561 words and the appropriate dictionaries were created. The phrases used in the measurement tests varied in length, ranging from simple phrases such as "How are you?" to more complex ones containing up to 25 words and several verbs along with subordination structures.

The results are shown in Table 1.1: 96% well translated words and 93.7% well translated and located inside the sentence, 15 words were added without affecting the understanding of the sentences, and 3 words were wrongly added affecting the meaning.

The results of the tests performed to check the translation speed of the system were also very satisfactory. The maximum time was 55 ms and the minimum 15 ms, 19.59 ms being the average for each sentence. These results allow our automatic translator to work in real-time systems.

1.4.2 Integration in the Maxine Animation Engine

The goal sought was to construct a translation module that could be integrated within another system that needed these translations in order to sign them.

Within our research group, an animation engine called Maxine [15] has been developed. This is a setting based on open source libraries capable of generating

Table 1.1 Quality measurements

Measurements	Results
Well translated words	539 (96%)
Words in correct order	526 (93.7%)
Unnecessary words but that not affect comprehension	15 (2.7%)
Unnecessary words that affect comprehension	3 (0.6%)

3D scenes in real time, which includes virtual actors to which different features have been added, such as animations, facial expressions varying according to mood, speaking and vocalizing capacity, the ability to modify tone according to mood or the capacity to perform presentations. At the present time, the Maxine system is based on the execution of commands, either introduced by the used or executed in *script* form. So, animation scripts is the method employed for word translation, although the switch to a different system for representing movements—one based on their parameters, such as other systems use—is being envisaged in order to be able to represent any sign. With the inclusion of this translation system from Spanish to LSE, a new "say this sentence in sign language" command has been created. Improvements in the capacities of this software for animating the orders extracted from the translator are presently underway. The system also includes a voice capture and text transformation module that produces valid input for the translation system, so that when integrated, it can reach the level of spoken sign language translated into text. As already mentioned, virtual actors possess moods which, when supplied to the translator, may influence the way the latter carries out translations, making these extremely dynamic and very similar to those performed by a human translator.

1.5 Conclusions and Future Work

In this chapter we present an automatic translator from spoken Spanish to Spanish Sign Language based on the use of grammatical and morphological rules, which allows translation of phrases in real time. It admits the input of phrases in written Spanish drawn from any system capable of generating them, and its output can be generated in different formats adaptable to animation generation systems. The system developed allows the inclusion of the interpreter's mood in such a manner that the signs obtained are modified depending on whether the interpreter is happy, angry, etc. The quality of the translations was validated only with teachers of sing language, but in the near future we expect to evaluate them by working with special education children schools.

In relation to technical future work, a very important line of research would be the one related to the expansion of the system's grammatical rules, in order to increase its translation capacity.

Acknowledgments   This project was partially funded by the Dirección General de Investigación: Project N° TIN2007-63025 and by the Government of Aragon: Walqa Agreement Ref. 2004/04/86 and Project N° CTPP02/2006. Authors thank the collaboration of the teachers from the Instituto María Moliner (Zaragoza, Spain) for the interpreter's sign language module.

References

1. *SIGNAR. Aprende lengua de signos española.* Fundación CNSE. Madrid.
2. Pérez, J, García, JM, Guillén, C, Sánchez, M, *Introducción a la lengua de signos española: una experiencia piloto*, Diego Martín (ed.). Murcia. 2001 (in Spanish)

3. Rodríguez MA, *Lenguaje de signos*. PhD Thesis. Madrid. 1992 (in Spanish)
4. http://personal2.redestb.es/martingv/ls.htm
5. http://www.planetavisual.net/right/diccio/index.htm
6. Bahngham, JA, Cox, SJ, Elliott, R, Glauert, JRW, Marshall, I, *Virtual Signing: Capture, Animation, Storage and Transmission – an Overview of the ViSiCAST Project*, IEEE Seminar on Speech and language processing for disabled and elderly people, 2000.
7. http://www.visicast.sys.uea.ac.uk
8. San-Segundo, R, Macías-Guarasa, J, Montero, JM, Fernández, F, *Translating Spoken Language into Sign Language*, GESTS, Vol. 13 (1), pp. 55–64, June 2005.
9. http://www.visicast.sys.uea.ac.uk/eSIGN/index.html
10. Safar, E, Marshall, I, *The architecture of an English-text-to-sign-languages translation system*, Recent Advances in Natural Language Processing, pp. 223–228, Sept 2001.
11. Ibáñez, E, Huerta, A, San-Segundo, R, D'Haro, LF, Fernández, F, Barra, R, *Prototipo de traducción de voz a lengua de signos española*. IV Jornadas en Tecnología del Habla, pp. 117–122, Nov 2006. (in Spanish).
12. IV Jornadas en Tecnologías del Habla, http://jth2006.unizar.es/Actas/4jth´actas.html *Libro de Actas*, 2006 (in Spanish).
13. *FreeLing*. http://garraf.epsevg.upc.es/freeling developed by the "Centro de Tecnologías y Aplicaciones del Lenguaje y del Habla", Universidad Politécnica de Cataluña, Spain.
14. *HamNoSys*. http://www.sign-lang.uni-hamburg.de/Projekte/HamNoSys/default.html
15. Baldassarri S, Cerezo E, Serón F, *Maxine: A platform for embodied animated agents.*, Computer & Graphics, 2008, to appear, doi:10.1016/j.cag.2008.04.006

Chapter 2
Influence of Binocular Disparity in Depth Perception Mechanisms in Virtual Environments

Matthieu Poyade, Arcadio Reyes-Lecuona, and Raquel Viciana-Abad

Abstract   In this chapter, an experimental study is presented for evaluating the importance of binocular disparity in depth perception within a Virtual Environment (VE), which is assumed to be critical in many manipulation tasks. In this research work, two assumptions are made: Size cues strongly contaminate depth perception mechanisms and binocular disparity optimizes depth perception for manipulation tasks in VE. The results outline size cues as possible cause of depth perception degradation and binocular disparity as an important factor in depth perception, whose influence is altered by the position within a VE.

2.1 Introduction

In certain industrial environments, the simulation of design and training processes is necessary and often involves manipulation tasks. Nevertheless, depending on the nature of the industrial task, the simulation of these processes under real world conditions may result limited and expensive due to logistical needs. In contrast, manipulation in Virtual Environments (VE) may become an interesting alternative to simulators based in real environments. Nowadays, technological improvements concerning virtual reality devices allow for the design of reliable simulations, easily reconfigurable and with a reasonable cost.

In the specific case of manipulation in VEs, the perception of depth is a decisive factor. The goal of this work is to provide a better understanding of depth perception mechanisms. The experimental study performed consists of two stages. First, the study evaluated the magnitude of sensorial conflicts generated by objects size in depth perception within a VE. Then, the study focused on the influence of binocular disparity in the process of depth perception.

M. Poyade (✉)
Departamentos de Technología Electrónica, ETSI de Telecomunicación Universidad de Málaga, Spain
e-mail: matthieu.poyade@uma.es

J.A. Macías et al. (eds.), *New Trends on Human–Computer Interaction*,
DOI 10.1007/978-1-84882-352-5_2, © Springer-Verlag London Limited 2009

2.2 Prior Work

Many studies have demonstrated the advantages of using stereoscopic visualization in VEs [1–4]. Stereoscopic cues provide a noteworthy improvement of depth perception in a very realistic way [5, 6], intensifying perception of surfaces and materials [7], and also facilitating spatial localization and navigation. Therefore, the already proved benefits of stereoscopic visualization support its implementation within VEs in which an accurate manipulation is required [3].

2.2.1 Depth Perception Mechanisms in Real World and Depth Cues Theory

Human visual system consists of very complex mechanisms, which are able to perform complex tasks, such as simultaneously processing two visual stimuli received from both eyes and generating a three-dimensional mental model. This mechanism is well known as stereopsis and it refers to the visual system capacity of computing coherently two monocular signals to create a three-dimensional view of an environment.

According to the literature, stereoscopic view depends on binocular and oculomotor depth cues [7]. Binocular depth cues refer to the depth sensation provided by the stereopsis by means of processing the slightly different retinal images of both eyes, resulting from the human eyes horizontal separation. It is commonly assumed that human eyes separation known as the average interocular distance, ranges from 6.3 cm to 6.5 cm [8]. Oculomotor depth cues comprise the sight accommodation and convergence processes [7].

Depth cues theory refers to depth provided not only by binocular and oculomotor depth cues but also by monocular depth cues. These last cues are known as pictorial cues and are related to depth information provided by images. The most common pictorial cues are occlusion, size, shade, illumination, texture, and color [6, 7].

The processing of depth cues by the visual system provides the sensation of depth related to an object and its surrounding. Many works [6, 9–11] suggested the study of depth perception taking into account both pictorial and stereoscopic (binocular and oculomotor) depth cues.

In a stereoscopically displayed VE, the control of the stereoscopic cues is essential in order to avoid sensorial conflicts due to accumulation of various cues.

2.2.2 Stereopsis and Depth Perception in a Virtual Environment

Depth Perception in Computer Generated Images (CGI) is strongly enhanced by stereoscopic vision. Furthermore, depth perception has demonstrated to improve when depth information is provided by various depth cues associated to stereopsis instead of only pictorial depth cues [7]. Therefore, the VE must provide the appropriate depth cues.

Pfautz suggested a stereoscopic visualization omitting eyes accommodation. Convergence is naturally performed at the focal distance of the observed virtual scene. Therefore, only binocular depth cues supply depth information.

Binocular depth cues ensure that each eye has its own viewpoint of the CGI displayed on the screen. The display system supplies the stereopsis by displaying twice each CGI considering a horizontal shift corresponding to the natural interocular distance. Perceived depth is illustrated in Fig. 2.1.

Fig. 2.1 Perceived depth in front of and behind the display panel.

Equations 1 and 2 respectively show the inner and outer perceived p depth from the projection area [12] as a function of the natural interocular distance e, the observation distance z and the displayed binocular disparity onto the screen d generated by the shifted CGI.

$$p = z/((e/d) + 1) \qquad (1)$$

$$p = z/((e/d) - 1) \qquad (2)$$

2.2.3 Stereoscopic Display Technical Principles

OpenGL libraries are very efficient in generating stereoscopic visualization in VE. These libraries allow for the use of several display functions [13, 14], such as the orthogonal projection function in symmetrical or asymmetrical perspective known as frustum which specifies the parameters of the camera attached to the user viewpoints in the VE. Both eyes are represented by two cameras horizontally shifted by the interocular distance.

Jones [12] and Holliman [15] proposed a method to convert depth between VE and real world depending on the parameters of the OpenGL display function.

Many works have focused on the study of the depth perception in VEs. Nevertheless, depth perception is still not well understood and is controlled with difficulty due to the numerous interactions between pictorial and stereoscopic cues.

Rosenberg [4] has experimentally studied the extent to which the interocular distance influences depth perception. He demonstrated the degradation of depth perception to be a function of interocular distance when this distance exceeds certain limitations of a broad range. Nevertheless, his experimental design consisted in a depth comparison of identical objects located close to the zero parallax plane. His results were obtained attending to depth information provided by binocular cues, but objects' size might have strongly affected this perception.

One of the main goals of this experimental study is the evaluation of the influence of certain pictorial depth cues regarding the interocular distance in depth perception. This experimental study is based on two hypotheses. The first hypothesis establishes that object size influences depth perception in a higher extent than stereoscopic depth cues, while manipulating objects of identical shape. The second hypothesis considers the existence of an optimal binocular disparity to accurately perceive depth in a VE.

2.3 Method

Fifteen volunteers (10 males, 5 females) were recruited from among students from the School of Telecommunication Engineering of the University of Malaga. Participants were aged from 22 to 27 ($\mu = 24$, $\sigma = 1.69$) and did not present any relevant visual deficiency. None of them were economically granted for his/her participation in this experiment.

The VE was implemented in Microsoft Visual C++ version 6.0 using the OpenGL libraries. Stereoscopic visualization was provided in the VE by using two asymmetrical oblique frustum functions shifted one from the other by the binocular distance, which was modified depending on the experimental conditions.

The experiment was performed on a PC (Pentium3 at 1 GHz, 1 GB RAM and graphic card INTENSE3D Wildcat Pro 4210 120 Hz) with a flat CRT screen IIyama Visión Master Pro 514 (width 300 mm, height 400 mm) customized for stereoscopic visualization using a CrystalEYES® workstation from StereoGraphics® corporation. The workstation consisted of a pair of standard LCD shutter glasses and an infrared emitter. CrystalEYES® shutter glasses provided to each eye its respective viewpoint of the VE displayed on the screen while the infrared emitter synchronized each viewpoint frequency to the half of the graphic card rendering frequency, i.e. at 60 frames per second.

2.3.1 Procedure

Participants were seated in front of the projection area at an approximate distance of 1 m. Their movements were restricted to the front of the display area. Interaction with the VE was based on virtual objects displacement using the keyboard. The screen was elevated in order to horizontally align participants' glance with the displayed virtual scene, as shown in Fig. 2.2a.

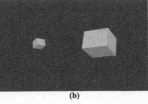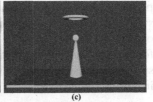

(a) (b) (c)

Fig. 2.2 (a) Installation of the experiment, (b) experimental design of the first stage, (c) experimental design of the second stage

Experimental design consisted of 15 scenarios which gathered different experimental conditions, according to a full factorial design, randomly ordered with an incomplete counter balanced design.

Before starting the experiment, participants performed a training trial in which they were asked to play with the virtual scene, by moving the virtual object inside and outside the screen. The objective was to detect whether they were affected by any visual disorder and also to get them familiarized with the stereoscopic display.

Then, participants received instructions concerning the aim of the experiment, design consideration (virtual objects may have different sizes) and temporal characteristics (duration: 35 minutes, 2 breaks strategically planned). Furthermore, they were informed about their right to rest whenever they wanted.

To evaluate participants' depth perception, the experiment consisted of different scenarios where they were asked to place an object at the same depth than a static reference. These scenarios were classified in two stages.

In the first experimental stage, the virtual scene consisted of two floating cubes colored and placed in a dark green background. The participants had to place the dynamic cube, located at their right side, at the same depth than the reference left object (see Fig. 2.2b). Movement of the cube was allowed in the Z-axis direction, inside and outside the screen, using the arrows keypad.

During the two sessions of this stage, depth perception was evaluated as a function of three factors (independent variables): the binocular disparity (0.0 cm, 1.0 cm, 3.0 cm, 6.4 cm, and 9.0 cm); the positions within the VE (inside the screen: -17.9 cm of perceived depth, at parallax zero: 0.0 cm of perceived depth, and outside the screen: 18.0 cm of perceived depth) and the objects' size (both objects sized equal, one object was twice bigger than the other one and vice versa).

In the second experimental stage, the graphical design was made in order to avoid any influence of objects size. Therefore, an important contaminant factor of depth perception was cancelled. In this stage, the task consisted in positioning two different objects at equal depth. Participants had to place a horizontally laid torus onto a cone-shaped object, in such a way that if the torus was released, it would fit perfectly onto the base of the cone-shaped object (see Fig. 2.2c). Participants could only move the torus following the Z-axis direction, inside and outside the screen, by pressing the arrows keypad. Again, participants' errors during the placement in depth of the torus were used to evaluate their depth perception. As in the first stage, position and binocular disparity were controlled as independent variables. In both stages, the dependent variable was the difference of depth between the manipulated object and the reference object (left side cube or cone). The computation of this difference was made when participants confirmed the object position by pressing the space bar. These differences were related to distances in the virtual world expressed in Virtual Units (VU).

2.4 Results

The experimental results were analyzed with a two way ANOVA (ANalysis Of VAriance) of repeated measures. Furthermore, this analysis was carried out considering three independent factors (object size, position, and binocular disparity) in the first stage of the experiment and two (position and binocular disparity) in the second stage. In both stages, the dependent variable was the difference of depth position between both objects within the VE, referred onwards as error measure.

2.4.1 Results of the First Stage

The error measure was strongly and significantly influenced by the size factor ($F_{(2,13)} = 28.789$, $p < 0.001$). As it was expected, when objects sized differently, error magnitude in the task of placement increased. Nevertheless, the influence of the binocular disparity factor ($F_{(4,11)} = 1.196$, $p < 0.366$) and the position factor ($F_{(2,13)} = 0.792$, $p < 0.474$) in the error measure were not found significant.

This analysis also revealed the existence of a significant interaction between size and position factors ($F_{(4,11)} = 7.734$, $p < 0.003$). Furthermore, the interaction between size and binocular disparity factors was also nearly significant.

Figure 2.3 shows the magnitude of the average error in the task of placing the virtual object in depth as a function of the three previously specified factors. As it can be seen in this figure, the difference in the depth position estimated between the dynamic object and the reference one was influenced by the difference in their sizes. Thus, the placement errors were of high magnitude and with a positive sign when the dynamic object was the biggest, while these errors were also of high magnitude but negatively signed when dynamic object was the smallest. So the participants unconsciously relied on the size cues to place dynamic objects. Moreover, the influence of the binocular disparity on the magnitude of the average error can also be seen in Fig. 2.3. Thus, the more the binocular disparity increased, the more the magnitude of the average error decreased. As well, the average error magnitude was more important in the case of further objects (Fig. 2.3a) than in the case of closer objects (Fig. 2.3.c).

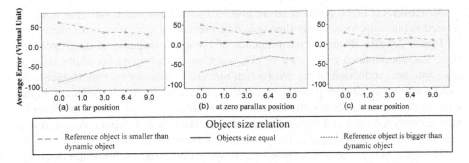

Fig. 2.3 Results of the first stage of the experiment. *Curves* representing the average error evolution in the task of placement in depth as a function of binocular disparity (expressed in cm) with different size relation

2.4.2 Results of the Second Stage

The analysis of the second stage revealed that both cues significantly influenced depth perception: position ($F_{(2,13)} = 10.853$, $p < 0.002$) and binocular disparity ($F_{(4,11)} = 9.710$, $p < 0.001$). Results also showed a significant interaction between both factors ($F_{(7,8)} = 7.567$, $p < 0.007$).

The influence of both factors in the error measure is shown in Fig. 2.4. Each curve shows the results for one of the three possible positions within the VE.

Fig. 2.4 Results of the second stage. *Curves* representing the average error in the task of placement in depth as a function of binocular disparity (expressed in cm) and position

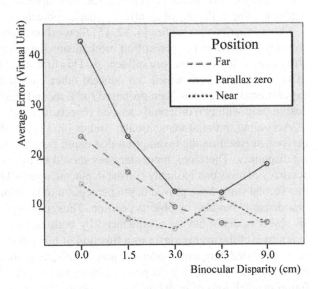

Results confirmed the high influence of binocular disparity cues. Regarding the influence of position, results logically revealed that the closer the virtual scene was located from the participant, the more effective was the placement.

Moreover, averaged position errors always showed a positive sign; participants tended to place the torus closer than the cone, presenting a constant error skew.

Figure 2.4 also illustrates the influence of binocular disparity in depth perception. Results obtained in the case of position close to zero parallax plane showed an asymptotic reduction in the error when binocular disparity increased. Hence in this condition, for disparity values higher than 3.0 cm the error got stabilized. In the case of distant and near position, there were optimal values of binocular disparity (respectively 6.4 cm and 3.0 cm). Therefore, a deterioration of depth perception was found when binocular disparity increased over this optimum.

However, in the case of near position, the error decreased for binocular disparity values higher than 6.4 cm. The reason is that participants compensated an experimental misconception by bringing back dynamic objects. Effectively, regarding the proposed depth information, participants tended to place dynamic objects beyond the allowed manipulation limits.

2.5 Discussion

In the first experiment stage, results have demonstrated the high influence of the objects size in mechanisms of depth perception in contrast with binocular disparity. These findings are in accordance with previous works which have also analyzed this influence [6, 16]. The analysis performed has revealed that objects size generates important errors in the perception of depth [16]. Thus, in the first stage of the experiment, participants' depth perception was built upon size cues and binocular cues neglected, due to the use of identically shaped objects.

Other experimental studies [4, 12, 15] focused on analyzing the influence of several depth cues in depth perception mechanisms have also carried out experiments without avoiding possible size influences. This first study has outlined the necessity of removing size cues which can conceal other cues influence. Therefore, a new experimental design has been proposed for a second stage of the experiment. This design dealt with two differently shaped objects to avoid size cues predominance.

According to the aforementioned studies [4, 12, 15], the second study has been performed based on the assumption that depth perception is influenced by binocular disparities. Therefore, binocular cues should be an important factor to improve accuracy of tasks that basically consist in placing a virtual object in depth. Results of this second study have proved depth perception to be influenced not only by binocular disparity but also by objects position. Thus, participants' average error placing an object in depth has been influenced by both factors. Differences found in the magnitude of the average error as a function of binocular disparity among positions have suggested that, with moderate values of disparity, the closer the objects are, the more accurate the depth perception is. Nevertheless, this last relation has not been found in conditions of high binocular disparity. Therefore, high values of binocular disparity do not guarantee an accurate depth perception. This last finding supports the idea of using lower anti-natural binocular disparity even if the VE is strongly distorted [4, 15].

The second experiment has also revealed that for objects placed close to the zero parallax plane, the depth perception error has tended asymptotically to a minimum value as the binocular disparity has been increased. This relation agrees with the results obtained by Rosenberg [4] in identical conditions. Nevertheless, Rosenberg has not considered the study of depth perception when objects were located further or closer than the zero parallax plane. In contrast with Rosenberg findings, in these last two cases, high values of binocular disparity have been found inefficient at improving accuracy of depth perception.

2.6 Conclusion

The understanding of depth perception mechanisms is a crucial issue to allow for accurate manipulation in a VE.

This work has evaluated the influence in depth perception of certain cues, such as size and binocular disparity. The size factor has been outlined as a possible cause of depth perception degradation. The findings presented substantiate that objects size strongly influences depth perception. Therefore, the analysis of the influence of other depth cues should be made avoiding this effect.

Previous studies have demonstrated binocular disparity as an important factor in depth perception. The analysis performed has also revealed that this influence is altered by the objects position. Thus, in case the virtual scene is located close to the zero parallax plane, an accurate perception of depth is ensured by a large range of binocular disparity values. Nevertheless, if the virtual scene is located much further or closer than the zero parallax plane, depth perception is accurate for binocular disparity included in a range slightly inferior to the natural eye separation.

Manipulating in depth in VEs is delicate and requires more investigation involving more participants. One possible approach of investigation relies on including proprioceptive and haptic cues to evaluate depth in a VE, by using haptic devices as manipulation interface.

Acknowledgments   This study has been partially funded by the Spanish Ministry of Education and Sciences (Project TIN2006-15202-C03-02) and the council of Andalusia (Group PAI TIC-171). Special thanks to Carmen Garcia Berdonés for her comments.

References

1. Alexander T et al. (2003) Depth perception and visual after-effects at stereoscopic workbench displays. Proc Virtual Real Annu Int Symp: 269–270
2. Bouguila L et al. (2000) Effect of Coupling Haptics and Stereopsis on Depth Perception in Virtual Environment. Proc. of the 1st Workshop on Haptic Human Computer Interaction: 54–62
3. Kim WS et al. (1987) Visual Enhancements in pick and place tasks: Human operators controlling a simulated cylindrical manipulator. IEEE J Rob Autom, RA-3: 418–425
4. Rosenberg L (1993) Effect of interocular distance upon operator performance using stereoscopic displays to perform virtual depth tasks. IEEE Annu Virtual Reality Int Symp: 27–32

5. Holliman N (2006) Three-Dimensional Display Systems. Handbook of Optoelectronics Vol II, Ed. Dakin JP and Brown RGW, Taylor & Francis, Boca Raton
6. Wanger LR et al. (1992) Perceiving spatial relationships in computer-generated images. IEEE Comput Graphics Appl, 12: 44–58
7. Pfautz JD (2002) Depth Perception in Computer Graphics. University of Cambridge. PhD Thesis http://www.cl.cam.ac.uk/techreports/UCAM-CL-TR-546.pdf. Accessed September 2002
8. Stanney KM et al. (1998) Human factors issues in Virtual Environments: A review of the literature. Presence Teleoper. Virtual Environ, 7: 327–351
9. Bülthoff HH and Mallot HA (1998) Integration of depth modules: stereo and shading. J Opt Soc Am A 5: 1749–1758
10. Guibal CR and Dresp B (2004) Interaction of color and geometric cues in depth perception: when does "red" mean "near"? Psychol Res, 69:30–40
11. Sinai MJ et al. (1998) Terrain influences the accurate judgment of distance. Nature, 395: 497–500
12. Jones G et al (2001) Controlling perceived depth in stereoscopic images. Proc. SPIE Int Soc Opt Eng, 4297: 42–53
13. Hearn D and Baker MP (1995) Gráficas Por Computadora con OpenGL. Prentice Hall, Madrid
14. Lipton L (1991) Stereographics, Developers Handbook. StereoGraphics Corp
15. Holliman N (2004) A mapping perceived depth to regions of interest in stereoscopic images. Proc. SPIE Int Soc Opt Eng, 5291: 117–128
16. Sweet BT and Kaiser MK (2006) Integration of size and binocular disparity visual cues in manual depth-control tasks. Coll. Technic. Papers. AIAA Model. Simulat Technol Conf 2006, 2: 933–957

Chapter 3
Semantic Web Interfaces for Newspaper Multimedia Content Management

Ferran Perdrix, Roberto García, Rosa Gil, Marta Oliva, and José A. Macías

Abstract   The S5T project explores the possibilities of a semantic content management system in the context of a mass media group (radio, TV, newspaper and internet). The system is based on Semantic Web technologies and attempts to build up a media repository that makes the media house more productive. To carry out such a challenge, the project features a user interface that takes profit from all the modelling and annotation effort, which is carried out during ontology construction and semantic annotation of audio transcriptions. In particular, three interfaces have been developed whose goal is to facilitate the main interaction modes, search and browsing. For the former, a query-by-example tool has been created. For the latter, there are two specialised interfaces, which allow browsing media contents and the semantic annotations for transcriptions. These interfaces make it possible to take profit from the underlying ontologies during user interaction.

3.1 Introduction

Recently, many newspaper companies are changing into news media houses. They own radio stations and video production parties that create content unsupported by traditional newspapers, but that they are able to be delivered by Internet newspapers. Web-based news publishing is evolving fast, as many other Internet services, and nowadays this service is trying to adapt information in manners that better fit user's interests and capabilities in the digital space.

F. Perdrix (✉)
Diari Segre. Del Riu 6, 25007 Lleida, Spain
e-mail: fperdrix@diarisegre.com

J.A. Macías et al. (eds.), *New Trends on Human–Computer Interaction*,
DOI 10.1007/978-1-84882-352-5_3, © Springer-Verlag London Limited 2009

The S5T[1] project is looking forward to producing more profit from news sites using cutting-edge ways to archive multimedia content based on Semantic Web technologies and human speech recognition. Previously, the Neptuno project [1] handled semantically enriched textual news and explored new capabilities in terms of information retrieval and content browsing. Now, in S5T, the objective is to expand this benefits to audio and audiovisual content in order to integrate the many kinds of multimedia content that are managed in a media house, such as radio or TV news.

In order to reuse existing semantic annotation tools and expand their benefits to audiovisual content, the approach followed in the S5T project is to transcribe the human speech present in the audio of radio and TV news. Once speech is recognized and transcribed as text, it is possible to annotate it reusing many of the tools in place for textual content.

Users exploit the new capabilities that the semantic web technologies provide while they search and browse the news repository in a transparent way. In order to accomplish this in a usable and accessible way, specialized user interfaces are required. Consequently, the aims of the S5T project range from aspects concerning content creation, indexation based on human speech and search to multimedia content visualization, assisted query authoring and browsing.

3.1.1 A Use Case

SEGRE[2] is a mass multimedia company that owns one TV channel, two radio stations, one newspaper and a web portal. SEGRE produces every day 64 newspapers pages, 8 hours of self-produced TV content, 24 hours of direct Radio emission and updates the web portal daily. Nowadays, contents are archived separately by media channel: TV, Radio, Internet, and newspaper. Identifying relationships among contents from different repositories is a cumbersome task, and the effort needed to manually integrate all these contents is not justifiable in terms of cost-benefit scale. Consequently, SEGRE is a good use case to test the improvements proposed in this project. SEGRE has a lot of content in several media: audio, video, text, etc. and can provide audience for the two groups of interest related to this project: journalists and end-users.

3.2 Architecture

The S5T project is based on domain conceptual models formalized using ontologies as it is shown on the left side of Fig. 3.1. Ontologies are used to annotate the digital contents managed by the system. In order to do this, a pre-processing task is carried

---

[1] Scaleable semantic personalised search of spoken and written contents on the Semantic Web (S5T), http://nets.ii.uam.es/~s5t
[2] Diari Segre Media Group, http://www.diarisegre.com

out with the aim of recognizing text from the audio part of audiovisual content. During the transcription, keywords are also detected and related to the ontology concepts using lexicons like WordNet [2].

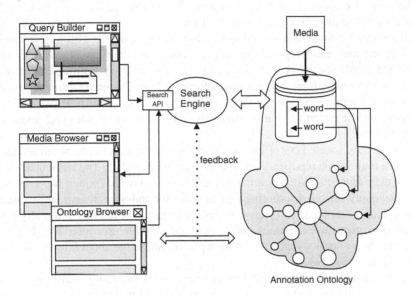

Fig. 3.1 System architecture

The transcription process makes it possible to integrate any kind of content with audio, and also to seamlessly integrate the annotation process with purely textual content. Then, semantic annotations make it possible to perform more accurate searches that take profit from the semantic relationship captured by the domain ontologies at place. There are more details about the transcription, ontology development and semantic annotation processes in [3].

However, in this chapter, the focus is placed on the left side of Fig. 1. The objective is to show how the underlying ontologies can be used in the user interface in order to provide a richer experience while maintaining its complexity low and avoiding usability looses. Otherwise, the lack of a user interface that takes profit from the domain knowledge as the users interact might make many of potential benefits unreachable as long users do not pose the semantic query in the right way.

3.3 Human–Semantic Web Interaction

One of the Human–Computer Interaction's great challenges has always been to change the way computer science was originally conceived, shifting from the primitive computer-centered conception to a brand new user-centered paradigm [4]. For instance, though the Semantic Web has been accepted as one of the most promising approaches to data integration and intelligent information processing, this cutting-edge technology is still out of the scope for most of the end-users. This is because users find it very difficult to learn and use applications based on Semantic Web technologies [5].

The core of these applications is perfectly functional and the main lack might be in their scalability. However, there is a clear lack of user interface tools and paradigms that facilitate, in a simple and usable way, to search and browse semantic metadata and the underlying web ontologies. Therefore, the Semantic Web can be considered usable just for skilled users, and even they find great difficulties as well [6]. In the S5T research project, we have adopted a User Centered Design approach that promotes putting the user in the center of the development process and tries to minimize their cognitive charge when interacting with ontologies and Semantic Web metadata.

First, we have focused our efforts on detecting the main user tasks when interacting with a multimedia repository and the underlying metadata. The main tasks, and also the main interaction modes, are query and browse. For the former, we propose a high-level query-intended authoring tool in order for end-users to extract and manage information easily. The objective is that users can pose queries in a really easy way using a query by example methodology and a usable user interface. They do not need to be an ontology-expert or have a priori knowledge about how the domain is structured.

On the other hand, there are two tools intended for browsing media as well as the semantic metadata and ontologies used to annotate it. The browsing approach is based on a methodology that attempts to facilitate browsing graph-data structures, like the Semantic Web, in a usable way. This methodology is detailed in the "Browsing Interface" section, where two user interfaces built on top of it are also presented. The first one is intended for browsing media and the audio transcriptions. The other one is intended for browsing the semantic annotations about media and their transcriptions, both the metadata and also the underlying ontologies.

S5T users start a typical interaction with the system by constructing a query that will allow retrieving the content they are interested in. The user receives assistance from the query authoring tool that guides him through the query construction phase. This allows end-users building advanced queries and to manage the available information to construct queries in an easy way. Once the query has been built and sent, the results are shown through the first navigation user interface, the one that presents audiovisual contents and is called the *Media Browser*. This interface shows the contents that have been selected by the query, their audio transcriptions and all the available editorial metadata (title, genre, type, etc.).

Audio transcriptions are enriched with links to the domain ontology for each of the detected keywords. These keywords are detected during the transcription process [3] and, when there is a corresponding concept in the domain ontology, a link is generated using a semantic annotation. The *Knowledge Browser*, the other browsing interface, allows users following this link and retrieves information about the concepts in the ontologies used for annotating content transcriptions. The whole knowledge structure can be browsed using this interface. For instance, a politics domain ontology for news about politics.

3.4 Query Authoring Tool

In order to reduce the gap between users and the semantic web, we provide end-users with the ability of querying and visualizing the existing knowledge available in our ontological media repository. To this end, we propose a low-abstraction-level WYSIWYG authoring tool supporting end-user-intended inference and automatic customization of the retrieved information, see Fig. 3.2. In our tool, a user with no programming-in-query-language skills can freely manipulate high-level representations of knowledge obtained from previous queries or simply from scratch.

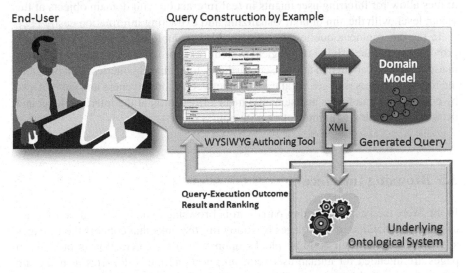

Fig. 3.2   Schema of the query authoring tool

Continuously, the system analyses the user's interaction and the underlying interface–domain information, which is automatically updated and maintained by the system from one session to another. By using a simple visual language, the user carries out graphical queries that the system automatically transforms into a XML query-like language, in order to be processed by the underlying ontological engine. The data obtained from the query execution is processed later on to obtain appropriate feedback and update the visual information on the environment, in order for the end-user to compose far more expressive queries visually.

We based on cutting-edge End-User-Development techniques such as Programming by Example [7], which consists in automatically generalizing programmatic output from examples that the user provides to the system. From this point of view, our system can be regarded as a query-by-example tool, but featuring further improvements with respect to traditional approaches.

Queries can be applied to a great deal of data models. Originally, they appeared 30 years ago, mostly related to relational databases where the main concern was to retrieve the best information possible in the shortest time [8]. Later on, query languages evolved from programmatic to other semantic notations, where the main concern was to help users compose queries easily, finally using authoring environments such as Microsoft Query-By-Example, which is based on a previous query-by-example notation developed by IBM [9]. Additionally, other existing notation languages are based on the object-oriented paradigm such as ConQuer [10] and GOQL [11], improving the expressiveness in information specification and retrieval with respect to the traditional relational model.

In our query-by-example tool, we leverage the semantic restrictions of previous models by using ontologies, which have proved to be rather flexible and expressive than other (object and relational) approaches. Our programming-by-example techniques allow for inferring user intents in real interaction with domain objects at the visual level, with the aim of both visualizing and extracting information easily [12].

In our environment, queries are composed by example when using the feedback provided by the underlying ontological system. This provides extra semantic information to reason about and assist users further while building queries. In a nutshell, the idea behind this is to get a real trade-off between expressiveness and easy-of-use by considering ontologies and semantic meta-information at the interface level and decreasing complexity in interacting with non-skilled.

3.5 Browsing Interface

In the Web, the basic interaction paradigm is browsing, which is based on the successive visualization of Web pages by following the links that connect them. Pages and links are the main building blocks upon which the interaction is built. Web pages are intended for human users consumption and methodologies to make the whole process usable and accessible are well established.

However, this browsing paradigm, and the principles to make the whole thing usable and accessible, cannot be directly applied to the Semantic Web. It is based on a different model, which is not based on pages and links. In the Semantic Web the fundamental block is the triple, composed by <subject, predicate, object>. This choice makes it clear that the Semantic Web was thought on different basis than the "classical" Web.

Triples are combined in order to build descriptions that try to capture the knowledge to be formalized. The combination of many triples builds up a graph; the Semantic Web data. Although the resulting model is easier to process by computers, the consumers of Semantic Web metadata are, at the end, human users. Consequently, usable and accessible interaction mechanisms are also required.

First of all, the basic browsing paradigm should change because the Semantic Web makes it very difficult to base the navigation on documents. In other word, to present to the user all the triples in a document as it is done in the Web. There is no presentation information and, what is more important, the amount of information in a single document can be too large, more than thousands of triplets. Moreover, the frontiers between documents are very fuzzy in the Semantic Web. Usually, many documents are combined in order to get coherent results as a unique graph. Thus, the problem here is where to put the limits when presenting semantic metadata to the user. In other words, how that piece is built and how new pieces are built and presented fulfilling user needs in order to build a browsing experience through the whole graph.

Semantic Web browsers like Tabulator [13] feature a more classical approach and show to the user all the triples from a Semantic Web document as an unfoldable tree. This approach embodies many usability problems because the tree grows rapidly and becomes difficult to manage. This is so because documents contain many triples and because each navigation step adds more triples from the new document to the current set.

Another approach is faceted browsing, like in /facet [14]. However, our preference is a simpler browsing mechanism that, though it might lack the guidance provided by facets, can deal better with heterogeneous information spaces. Moreover, it is not clear how systems like /facet deal with metadata structures that feature many anonymous resources, as it is the case for the semantic metadata managed in the S5T project.

In order to facilitate browsing, the S5T approach is based on the construction of graph fragments [15]. Following this approach, it is possible to construct coherent fragment for a graph starting from any graph node that is not anonymous. For instance, for the metadata that describes a piece of content, the starting point is the node that represents it and that is the subject for all the triples that describe it. This node has an ID and consequently is not anonymous.

All the triples that start from this node are part of the fragment. To this set, all the triples that describe objects that are anonymous are also added. This happens for all nodes that are only identifiable in the context of the starting node. For instance, for metadata describing a piece of content and the corresponding audio segment generated during the transcription process, the segments do not have an identifier and thus their descriptions will be included in the fragment describing the content item.

Consequently, all the triples that describe anonymous items are also in the fragment. This way, it is possible to construct coherent fragments that become the browsing steps. From a fragment, it is possible to follow the next browsing step starting from the triple objects that are not anonymous. The process continues iteratively and interactively, the metadata describing the selected identified node is retrieved and the fragment is built.

For instance, the user might want to get a description of the genre attribute. Therefore, he triggers a new browsing step, e.g. by clicking the genre URI, and the metadata describing it is retrieved from the IPTC News Codes Subjects Ontology[3] showing that the genre label is "politics" and some additional metadata about it.

Moreover, in order to make the results more usable, when they are rendered as interactive HTML the fragments are augmented with all the available labels and

---

[3]http://rhizomik.net/ontologies/2006/01/NewsCodes-SubjectsOnto.owl

titles for all the appearing URIs. For instance, the left part of Fig. 3.3 shows the HTML rendering for some metadata fragments. As it can be observed, the URI for the genre value has been replaced by the label specified for its URI.

3.5.1 Media Browser

Once the query is executed, results are shown by the *Media Browser*. This interface allows navigating through the multimedia pieces selected by the query and presents the available RDF metadata describing them. These descriptions are based on a generic rendering of RDF data as interactive HTML for increased usability [15]. Figure 3.3 shows a view of the Media Browser interface. On the left, there are the renderings for the metadata fragments describing the retrieved contents. On the right, there is a specialized audiovisual view that renders the content, audio and video, and allows interacting with it through a click-able version of the audio transcription.

.../20070113.mp3 a AudioType	
title	Butlletí Nit
date	2007-01-13
genre	politics
	Referrers

http://www.segre.com/audio/20070113.mp3

La mobilització en contra dels transgènics i en favor de Josep Pàmies també ha servit per introduir altres reclamacions. En aquest cas, alguns dels col·lectius de la lluita contra aquests cultius demanen que la Universitat de Lleida rebi una especia-

Fig. 3.3 Media Browser presenting content metadata (*left*) and the annotated transcription (*right*)

Two kinds of interactions are possible from the transcription. First, it is possible to click on any word in the transcription that has been indexed in order to perform a keyword-based query for all content in the database where that keyword appears.

Second, the transcription is enriched with links to the ontology used for semantic annotation. Each word in the transcription whose meaning is represented by an ontology concept is linked to a description of that concept, which is shown by the Knowledge Browser detailed in the next section. The whole interaction is performed through the user web browser using AJAX in order to improve the interactive capabilities of the interface.

For instance, the transcription includes the name of a politician that has been indexed and modeled in the ontology. Consequently, it can be clicked in order to get all the multimedia content where the name appears or, alternatively, to browse all the knowledge about that politician encoded in the corresponding domain ontology.

3.5.2 *Knowledge Browser*

This interface allows users browsing the knowledge structures used to annotate content. The same RDF data to HTML rendering used in the Media Browser is also used in the Knowledge Browser. Each browsing step through the ontologies is based on interactive metadata fragments like the one shown in Fig. 3. Consequently, continuing with the politician example in the previous section, when the user looks for the available knowledge about that person, an interactive view of the RDF data modeling him is shown.

This way, the user can take profit from the modeling effort and, for instance, be aware of the politician's party, that he is a member of the parliament, etc. This interface constitutes a knowledge browser so the link to the parliament can be followed and additional knowledge can be retrieved, for instance a list of all the members of the parliament.

In addition to this recursive navigation of all the domain knowledge, at any browsing step, it is also possible to get all the multimedia content annotated using the concept currently being browsed. This action would bring the user back to the Media Browser. Thanks to this dual browsing experience, the user can navigate through audiovisual content using the *Media Browser* and through the underlying semantic models using the *Knowledge Browser* in a complementary an inter-weaved way. Moreover, as for the *Media Browser*, the *Knowledge Browser* is also implemented using AJAX so the whole interactive experience can be enjoyed using a web browser.

3.6 Conclusions and Future Work

The objective of the S5T project is to integrate different kinds of content through semantically annotated audio transcriptions. Annotations are based on semantic metadata and ontologies. The challenge is then to provide user interfaces that allows user, which are newspaper workers not skilled in Semantic Web tools, to interact with content and annotations in an efficient and effective way.

The main interaction modes are query and browsing. For the former, a query-by-example tool has been developed. On the other hand, two specialized interfaces have also been developed in order to facilitate media and semantic metadata browsing. The browsing experience is rooted on a metadata graph fragmentation approach. The *Media Browser* is based on this browsing mechanism and allows navigating multimedia content and also semantic annotations.

Keywords in the transcription are linked to the domain ontology concepts that capture their semantics. This link can be followed using the second specialized interface, the *Knowledge Browser*. This second kind of browsing allows users to take profit from the knowledge formalized by the underlying ontologies. Both browsing mechanisms, the one through media and the one through knowledge, can be combined in order to provide a richer browsing experience.

Future work concentrates on integrating the user interfaces with the rest of the S5T components. The next step is to perform exhaustive user tests of the whole system. However, our long-term goal is to make the query and browsing tools also available for newspaper end-users. On the other hand, we are also exploring an interface for assisted metadata edition that will allow journalists editing semantic annotations and ontologies. Semantic forms are used for this purpose and are also based on the RDF to HTML rendering.

Acknowledgments The work described in this chapter has been partially supported by the Ministerio de Educación y Ciencia under the Programa Nacional de Tecnologías Informáticas, S5T project (TIN2005-06885).

References

1. Castells, P., Perdrix, F., Pulido, E., Rico, M., Benjamins, R., Contreras, J., et al. Newspaper Archives on the Semantic Web. In Navarro-Prieto, R., Lorés, J. (eds.): HCI related papers of Interacción 2004, Springer Verlag (2006) 267–276
2. Fellbaum, C. WordNet: An Electronic Lexical Database. MIT Press (1998)
3. Tejedor, J., García, R., Fernández, M., López, F., Perdrix, F., Macías, J.A., Gil, R., Oliva, M., Moya, D., Colás, J., Castells, P. Ontology-Based Retrieval of Human Speech. In Proceedings of the 6th International Workshop on Web Semantics, WebS'07. IEEE Computer Society Press (2007)
4. Shneiderman, B. Leonardo's Laptop. MIT Press (2003)
5. Shadbolt, N., Berners-Lee, T., Hall, W. The Semantic Web revisited. IEEE Intelligent Systems, Vol. 21, No. 3 (2006) 96–101
6. Heath, T., Domingue, J., Shabajee, P. User interaction and uptake challenges to successfully deploying Semantic Web technologies. In Proceedings of the 3rd International Semantic Web User Interaction Workshop, Athens, Georgia, USA (2006)
7. Lieberman, H. (ed.) Your Wish Is my Command: Programming by Example. Morgan Kaufmann Publishers. Academic Press, USA (2001)
8. Ozsoyoglu, G. Example-Based Graphical Database Query Languages. IEEE Computer (1993)
9. Zloff, M.M. Query-by-Example: A Data Base Language. IBM Systems Journal, Vol. 16, No. 4 (1977) 324–343
10. Bloesch, A.C., Halpin, T.A. ConQuer: a conceptual query language. In Proceedings of the International Conference on Conceptual Modeling, LNCS, Vol. 1157. Springer-Verlag (1996) 121–33
11. Keramopoulos, E., Pouyioutas, P., Sadler, C. GOQL, A Graphical Query Language for Object-Oriented Database Systems. BITWIT (1997)
12. Macías, J.A. and Castells, P. Providing End-User Facilities to Simplify Ontology-Driven Web Application Authoring. Interacting with Computers. The Interdisciplinary Journal of Human-Computer Interaction. Elsevier. Vol. 20, No. 1, January (2008) 29–47
13. Berners-Lee, T., et al. Tabulator: Exploring and Analyzing linked data on the Semantic Web. In Proceedings of the 3rd International Semantic Web User Interaction Workshop, Athens, USA (2006)
14. Hildebrand, M., van Ossenbruggen, J., Hardman, L. /facet: A Browser for Heterogeneous Semantic Web Repositories. In Proceedings of the International Semantic Web Conference 2006, LNCS, Vol. 4273. Springer-Verlag (2006) 272–285
15. García, R., Gil, R. Improving Human–Semantic Web Interaction: The Rhizomer Experience. CEUR Workshop Proceedings, Vol. 201 (2006) 57–64

Chapter 4
Designing an Interactive Installation for Children to Experience Abstract Concepts

Anna Carreras and Narcís Parés

Abstract In this chapter we present the design process followed for an interactive experience in a museum installation for children of age 14 to 18. The experience wishes to communicate a set of abstract concepts through full-body interaction following the interaction-driven design strategy. We also present a design framework that we have derived from the design process of this and previous full-body interactive experiences, in an attempt to generalize the steps we have followed. This framework is based on five levels, namely: conceptual, symbolic, semantic, user attitude, and user action levels. We believe this will allow designers to achieve experiences that better communicate abstract concepts and notions through interaction itself by making the users "live" the experiences in their own flesh through full-body interaction.

4.1 Introduction

There is a huge diversity in projects that use technology to engage children in learning, or creative activities. These projects approach the transmission of specific knowledge of concrete areas rather than abstract concepts. Interaction design of informal learning applications has focused on ways to bring technology into children's learning activities rather than focusing on the design of children's experience. This approach fails to exploit the intrinsic characteristics of interactive media and to propose novel forms of interaction. Most applications are also focused on creating learning applications based on school curricula using interaction to transmit a very specific content with very specific support material [3]. These applications are designed to present information using interaction as a mere tool to access the

A. Carreras (✉)
Institut Universitari de l'Audiovisual, Universitat Pompeu Fabra. Tànger 135. 08018
Barcelona, Spain
e-mail: acarreras@iua.upf.edu

J.A. Macías et al. (eds.), *New Trends on Human–Computer Interaction*,
DOI 10.1007/978-1-84882-352-5_4, © Springer-Verlag London Limited 2009

information stored and focused on task-based activities which are largely passive [13]; i.e. they are only based on information retrieval paradigms.

Few attempts have been undertaken [17, 18, 15] to approach installations that explore interaction properties or that build frameworks for such experiences, resulting in a lack of contributions in this area as pointed out by Jensen and Skov [6]. For example, they use interactive technologies as the tool to propose new approaches to knowledge that can be as abstract as learning about systems and robotics [16, 19, 15] or more concrete [17, 7, 8]. Others use new pervasive technologies to facilitate new forms of exploration [14, 5, 20].

However, an improvement in the understanding of interaction and its properties should help better design motivating experiences for children and decide when interaction is useful and justified to use for learning [9, 4]. The development of playful interactive installations for children offers an opportunity to better understand some properties of interaction itself and has informed us to define design guidelines which can be used for future applications. Our main goal when developing interactive installations for children is that we want to enrich their playful experience with interaction in a way that could not be achieved with any other media.

Therefore, our approach focuses on interaction design. We propose to study the characteristics of media, the used interfaces and the guidelines that can lead us to build experiences to transmit very general abstract concepts. This complementary approach focuses on user attitudes that can be finally understood as the base of the experience from which knowledge is gained.

In this chapter we present the design guidelines followed to develop a multi-user interactive playful installation, specially conceived for children, where full-body interaction helps participants experience how science is structured while promoting participation among users.

4.2 Connexions

Connexions is an installation conceived for Barcelona's Science Museum "Cosmo-Caixa." Based on previous work [11, 10] full-body user actions and attitudes are designed to make participants experience and understand the idea that science is a network of knowledge, with interrelated areas, where cooperation between scientists is essential for its evolution. This is achieved by:

- Designing the installation (the game play, the interactions, the concepts to be experienced, etc.) to fit the context where it is placed.
- Defining actions within user interaction that support very specific user activities. These activities structure user attitudes that promote an adequate experiencing of the abstract concepts we want to communicate.
- Understanding the concepts experienced through perception-action interactions with the environment as gained knowledge [2].

4.2.1 The Context: The Museum

The central strategy underlying museology in "CosmoCaixa" is based on showing the visitor that all areas in scientific knowledge are related to each other. Therefore, experiments, real pieces, and living beings are placed in one single large exhibit (3500 m^2) called the "room of matter." This room is structured in four areas that follow evolution of matter since the beginning of the Universe:

- Inert matter: e.g. radiation and waves, optics, fluids, uncertainty;
- Living matter: e.g. genes and genetics, the cell, the first ecosystems;
- Intelligent matter: e.g. the neuron, perception;
- Civilized matter: e.g. tools, fire, self-awareness, inventing matter.

"CosmoCaixa" takes selected objects (e.g., a fossil, a meteorite, a brain, a living fish, etc.) as the excuse from which to guide the visitor into scientific knowledge, as opposed to subdividing the museum into isolated compartments (e.g., mechanics, optics, waves, etc.) as traditional science museums have done in the past. In other words, each object represents a set of scientific domains that are related to it and by interesting the visitor in the object she is then engaged in the concepts behind the object (right half of Fig. 4.1, museologic approach).

Fig. 4.1 Underlying museology strategy for "CosmoCaixa" and the related strategy for the interactive experience

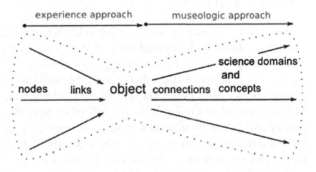

Because we wanted to stress that scientific areas are not isolated compartments, we decided to use the notion of a mesh or network as the leading metaphor to design the installation. This linked with the museological approach of "CosmoCaixa" in an inverse direction (left half of Fig. 4.1, experience approach). In other words, the interactive experience starts from scientific concepts and domains and leads to discovering a related (virtual) object; that virtual object then represents one of those found in the museum that links back to the scientific fields.

4.2.2 Game Play

Connexions, is a full body interactive installation for children of 14 to 18 years old. The virtual environment is projected onto the floor surface that acts as a large screen, 5 m × 3.8 m (Fig. 4.2a). The VE is a mesh composed of nodes that are interlinked in the fashion of a neural net. All this net is based on shades of gray on a white background. A subset of nodes (four to nine) are highlighted and labeled with a tag that is taken from a concept found within the museum's textual displays of the exhibited objects. Some of the highlighted nodes are clearly interrelated through their tags and refer to one specific object in the museum, while the remaining nodes are not related to that object. For example, the concepts—"atmosphere," "fusion," "turbulence," "trajectory," "solar system origin" and "extraterrestrial stone"—refer to a "meteorite" object. These are mixed with two more concepts; "genes" and "floatability," that have no relation with the meteorite.

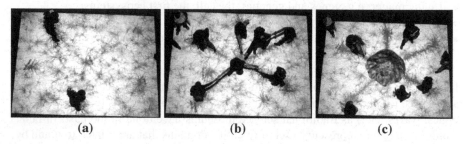

(a)   (b)   (c)

Fig. 4.2 Game play. (**a**) children activate (color) nodes by standing on them, (**b**) children link activated nodes connecting their bodies, (**c**) an object (here a meteorite) appears when children link all the nodes related to it

By walking around the space, children explore the mesh and may discover they can activate those nodes related to the object by standing on them. Activation of the nodes is represented by them acquiring a color (different for each node) showing that the concept is related to the others and to the "hidden" object (Fig. 4.2a). The non-related nodes cannot be activated by users. Children may make the activated nodes to grow colored extending links towards other activated nodes. They can achieve this by expanding their bodies along these paths, e.g. by extending their arms or legs in different directions to test where the links grow. The goal of the activity is that children link all nodes with the predefined coloured paths so that a specific network of nodes is completed. The virtual linkage of the nodes is performed by the physical linkage of the children's bodies: holding hands, extending their legs or arms, touching each other, etc. (Fig. 4.2b), hence embodying the metaphor of the mesh or network that acts as an allegory for the structure of science. When all the nodes that make reference to the hidden object are linked, a virtual 3D image of the object appears (Fig. 4.2c). A group of 8 to 15 children are necessary to activate and link the nodes and discover the objects. After the object is discovered and shown for a while, the experience restarts with a new set of nodes, concepts and hidden object.

4.3 Interaction Design

As said above, the goal of the experience was to transmit to children the abstract notion of science being a network of knowledge that interconnects concepts and domains.

4.3.1 Interaction-Driven Strategy: The Framework

To develop such an application our design is based on the interaction-driven design methodology [12]. This is achieved by concentrating on how the users are to interact with it, which actions they will perform and which attitudes they will experience.

Interaction-driven design is a strategy to develop interactive experiences that starts from defining user attitudes, as opposed to the idea of developing experiences through a content-driven approach, where a predefined content guides the way the application presents it to the users. Hence, our approach focuses precisely on interactivity and the actions and attitudes that users adopt in a certain experience, analyzing the interaction with the elements, and the participation of the user in such a way that the obtained results allow the emergence of the topic of the application.

Following the interaction-driven strategy user actions are placed at the centre of the experience design. The idea that interaction itself can generate meaning emerges from the design process that is followed, focusing on the relationship between the activities and attitudes of users within interaction and the concepts or ideas that we wish to communicate.

4.3.2 Full-Body Interaction

Our interaction approach is based on full-body interaction. This type of interaction provides a very good support for generating meaning through user attitudes. In effect, gestures and body movement usually provide very clear notions of an attitude. By presenting the real-time generated stimuli at a human scale, we provide an excellent context to develop user attitudes and hence generate meaning within the interactive experience.

Full-body interactions propose novel forms to interact with the virtual environment, in contrast to the desktop style, and promotes user activity (as opposed to passivity). This approach poses some interesting questions, such as: which actions and behaviors of the user should be considered for the game? what kind of interfaces should be used to support these actions and behaviors?

In order to give the participants freedom of physical action and not encumber them we propose to work with non-invasive interfaces to capture users' full-body behaviors.

Concerning game design this approach allows the game designers to achieve the following goals:

- Include more actions and activities to the game play and explore richer communicative dialogs.
- Users need not wear any sensors, cables or markers, making the installation extremely accessible to all sorts of public. This improves the throughput of users since they do not need to dress themselves up with sensing gear before they start the experience.

- By using non-invasive systems and analyzing the best structure for the interactive activity, a natural full-body interaction is reached and users can approach the installation and start interacting right away.
- Non-invasive systems and especially artificial vision systems achieve an interaction without having to manipulate physical elements, hence maximizing robustness and minimizing maintenance.

4.3.3 Multiuser Games

Apart from promoting activity among users by designing full-body interaction, for the interactive game to explore more participative structures we propose games with an inherently multiuser structure, i.e. the game goal is impossible to attain without collaboration with other participants.

This also adds some secondary goals to the transmission of meaning:

- The experience promotes interaction among users. It enhances collaboration and facilitates a high multiuser instantaneous capacity.
- The game is inherently participative, promoting socialization among users, who may comment on their experience in real time.
- The design of game interactions with multiuser structure and full-body interactions allows designers to think about richer and more complex actions for the users to perform.

4.3.4 Model for Meaning Generation

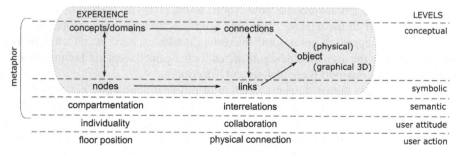

Fig. 4.3 Model describing the relations on which interaction design is supported (see text for details)

To design applications with the structure and properties described above and with the main goal of transmitting abstract concepts we propose a model based on five levels, namely conceptual, symbolic, semantic, user attitude, and user action (Fig. 4.3). The model helps designers to establish the rules of the game and the interactive output responses – the most concrete level in the model – by analyzing the meaning that they wish to communicate – the most abstract level in the model:

1. *Conceptual-semantic relation*: The meaning (the abstract notions to be transmitted to the users) constitute the conceptual level, the upper level of the model. The conceptual level is related to the semantic level, where the main abstract concepts that represent the desired meaning are chosen. The relation to the semantic level is established by relating the notions to meanings, in this case the notion of "concepts and domains" to the (semantics) meaning of "compartmentation" and relating the notion of "connections" (of those "concepts and domains") to the meaning of "interrelations" between compartmented items.

2. *Semantic-symbolic relation, the metaphor*: To transmit the desired meaning to the users, a metaphor is chosen for the interaction design, as well as for the design of the response (stimuli) of the experience, no matter whether the feedback is a visual response, sound, etc. The metaphor introduces symbolic elements to represent the concepts of the semantic level which, at the same time, are related to the conceptual level, hence, bringing together all the three top levels of the model. In Connexions, the chosen metaphor is that of a "mesh" or "network," relating "compartmentation" with the visual notion of a node in the network, and "interrelations" with the visual links of the mesh.

3. *Interaction design, a user attitude for the symbols*: This is the central focus of our research, i.e. to design user attitudes that can support the semantics of the experience. Each user, as an individual, is related to the notion of "nodes" at the symbolic level. Therefore, "individuality" signifies "compartmentation." Likewise, a "collaborative attitude" is related to the notion of "links," which signifies "interrelations."

4. *User activity, enhancing user attitude*: In this level the actions are designed for the experience activity to promote the users to adopt certain attitudes. In other words, if a user must fulfill the act of "individuality," she must move through space inputting her position to the system. On the other hand, to generate a "collaborative attitude," users must physically connect with others. These actions are physically conveying the metaphor.

4.3.5 Communication of Meaning

To sum up the described levels and the diagram (Fig. 4.3) the bottom-up steps taken by users in interaction are a set of actions that promote two attitudes, namely individuality and collaboration. Through individuality, they activate the nodes (the visual output of the metaphor), which provides the meaning of compartmented science domains. However, through collaboration, they make branches grow between nodes until they are all connected, which generates the meaning of interrelations between domains. Moreover, this collaboration also directly signifies collaboration between scientists in finding new connections in knowledge and, hence, new discoveries. Attitudes and actions are designed with the common goal of promoting the desired physical full-body interaction, which will make participants experience while playing the desired abstract meaning.

When the virtual object appears, children can reevaluate the actions they just performed, the consequences of their attitudes, and question themselves about the relations:

- Between the object and the concepts in the activated and linked nodes (Fig. 4.4).
- Between their activity during interaction and the obtained results.

This minimum notions provided to the children that pass through the experience were designed to avoid making the activity meaningless [1].

Fig. 4.4 Users collaborating linking together (two views)

4.4 Results

We have gathered data through pre and post surveys to groups of children visiting Barcelona's Science Museum, "CosmoCaixa" and experiencing Connexions installation (144 users surveyed). The survey was based on questions with scale-based answer related to ease of use and enjoyment, and questions with free answer related to the meaning of the experience. We have also surveyed 68 children that visit the museum but do not play with the installation, as control groups. Participants experiencing the installation have reported us how they enjoy the experience and they show an improvement, from pre to post, in their answers about the connection of domains in science.

However, we found no statistical significant improvement between those that experienced the installation with respect to the control groups that only learned about these concepts through the guided visit to the museum. This has to be further researched in future observations and data collection. This could be so due to the excellent effort in museology that "CosmoCaixa" has invested on in its last restructuring. It could also be partially due to the fact that these youngsters are given the questionnaires when about to leave the museum and might not take good care in answering them. We must strengthen the experimental set-up for future editions.

On the other hand, the constructivist approach believes that the knowledge gained through experience is brought up in the person's analysis of new experiences in the long run and, perhaps, our survey to the youngsters at such short time after the experience might still not reflect them having gained this knowledge. In any case, we can say that our installation does help communicate these concepts since the difference from pre to post test shows a significant improvement. Therefore we have produced an experience that, regarding current findings, is at least as good as other methods.

4.5 Conclusions

Our main conclusion is that when designing interaction that wishes to generate meaning, a good approach is to focus on the relationship between the activities and attitudes of users within interaction and the concepts or ideas that are to be transmitted. Users' actions must be placed at the centre of the design and the meaning must be generated by making the users live the concepts through designing accurately their attitudes. Knowledge can be then gained through the proposed interaction and interface through users' actions, their perceptions and the reflexions about the result of their actions. This novel approach of human–computer interaction as a communication medium through experience design can be further researched and extended to many other cases to be able to structure it formally and learn more about the potential of interaction and its capability to transmit abstract meaning.

Acknowledgments   We thank Barcelona's Science Museum "CosmoCaixa" and especially its pedagogical team for their support and confidence in Connexions project.

References

1. Ackerman (1993) Tools for constructive learning: On Interactivity. Proceedings of International Federation for Information Processing.
2. Benyon, D., Pasquinelli, E. (2006) Enaction and the concept of Presence. In Proceedings of the International Conference on Enactive Interfaces, 22–23.
3. Davies, C., Hayward, G., and Lukman, L. (2004) 14–19 and Digital Technologies: A review of research and projects. Futurelab Literature reviews.
4. Druin, A., Inkpen, K. (2001) When are Personal Technologies for Children? In Personal and Ubiquitous Computing, 5(3), 191–194.
5. Facer, K., Joiner, R., Stanton, D., Reid, J., Hull, R., and Kirk, D. (2004) Savannah: Mobile Gaming and Learning? Journal of Computer Assisted Learning, 399–409.
6. Jensen, J.J., Skov, M.B. (2005) A review of research methods in children's technology design. In Proceeding of Interaction Design and Children, 80–87.
7. Johnson, A. Roussos, M. Leigh, J. Vasilakis, C. Barnes, C. Moher, T. (1998) The NICE project: learning together in a virtual world. Proceedings IEEE of the Virtual Reality Annual International Symposium.

8. Ohlsson S., Moher T., Johnson A. (2000) Deep Learning in Virtual Reality: How to Teach Children that the Earth Is Round. In Proceedings Annual Meeting of the Cog. Sci. Soc.
9. Papert, S. (1980) Mindstorms: Children, Computers, and Powerful Ideas. Basic Books.
10. Parés, N., Carreras, A., Durany, J. (2005) Generating meaning through interaction in a refreshing interactive water installation for children. In Proceedings of Interaction Design and Children 2005, ACM Press.
11. Parés, N., Carreras, A., Durany, J., Ferrer, J., Freixa, P., Gomez, D., Kruglanski, O., Parés, R., Ribas, J.I., Soler, M., Sanjurjo, A. (2006) Starting Research in Interaction Design with Visuals for Low Functioning PAS Children. CyberPsychology & Behavior. Mary Ann Liebert, Inc. publishers, New Rochelle, NY. Vol 9.2, 218–223.
12. Parés, N., Parés, R. (2001) Interaction-driven virtual reality application design. A particular case: "El Ball del Fanalet or Lightpools". Presence: Teleoperators and Virtual Environments. Cambridge, MA: MIT Press. Vol. 10, 2, 236–245.
13. Price, S., Rogers, Y. (2004) Let's get physical: the learning benefits of interacting in digitally-augmented physical spaces. Computers & Education, Vol. 43, 137–151.
14. Price, S., Rogers, Y., Stanton, D., Smith, H. (2003) A new conceptual framework for CSCL: Supporting diverse forms of reflection through multiple interactions. CSCL Conference.
15. Resnick, M. Berg, R., Eisenberg, M. (2000) Beyond Black Boxes: Bringing Transparency and Aesthetics Back to Scientific Investigation. Journal of the Learning Sciences.
16. Resnick, M. and Silverman, B. Some Reflections on Designing Construction Kits for Kids. Proceedings of Interaction Design and Children conference, Boulder, CO. (2005).
17. Rogers, Y., Scaife, M., Gabrielli, S., Smith, H. and Harris, E. (2002) A Conceptual Framework for Mixed Reality Environments: Designing Novel Learning Activities for Young Children. In Presence Teleoperators and Virtual Environments. Vol. 11, 6, 677–686.
18. Roussou, M. (2004) Learning by Doing and Learning Through Play: an exploration of interactivity in virtual environments for children. In Computers in Entertainment, vol. 2, 1, section: Virtual reality and interactive theaters, ACM Press.
19. Weal, M., Cruickshank, D., Michaelides, D., Millard, D., De Roure, D., Hornecker, E., Halloran, J. and Fitzpatrick, G. (2006) A reusable, extensible infrastructure for augmented field trips. In Proceedings of 2nd IEEE International Workshop on Pervasive ELearning, 201–205.
20. Zuckerman, O., Resnick, M. (2003) System Blocks: A Physical Interface for System Dynamics Learning. In Proceedings International Conference of the System Dynamics Society.

Chapter 5
Design of Videogames in Special Education

J.L. González Sánchez, M.J. Cabrera, F.L. Gutiérrez, N. Padilla Zea, and P. Paderewski

Abstract The use of new technological and learning methods that help to improve the learning process has resulted in the inclusion of the video games as active elements in the classrooms. Videogames are ideal learning tools since they provide training skills, promote independence and increase and improve students' concentration and attention. For special education students with learning difficulties, it is very important to adapt the game to each student's cognitive level and skills. New game technologies have helped to create alternative strategies to increase cognitive skills in the field of Special Education. This chapter describes our experience in video games design and in new forms of human–computer interaction addressed to develop didactic games for children with communication problems such as autism, dysphasia, ictus or some types of cerebral paralysis.

5.1 Introduction

Nowadays the attention to people with special needs, in particular those with communication disabilities is an area in continuous expansion in our society. Hence, it is very important to develop technological solutions for the rehabilitation and integration of people with communication difficulties, regardless of their problems (paraplegia, cerebral palsy, autism, etc.).

Humans, throughout history, have had the ability to manage their leisure time and have used this factor as cultural development. According to Huizinga [1], the game with the relationship and abilities that humans acquire with the playing process is one of the most important aspects in the human social-cultural evolution. Videogames are 21st century games and they are an attractive platform to children. They provide interesting human–computer interaction methods to enrich the

J.L. González Sánchez (✉)
Videogames and E-Learning Research Lab (LIVE) – GEDES. Software Engineering Department, University of Granada, C/ Daniel Saucedo Aranda, s/n, E-18007, Granada, Spain
e-mail: joseluis@ugr.es

J.A. Macías et al. (eds.), *New Trends on Human–Computer Interaction*,
DOI 10.1007/978-1-84882-352-5_5, © Springer-Verlag London Limited 2009

learning process in special education. Moreover, games help to improve social relationships, to raise the communication level and to ease the assimilation of new concepts that improve the learning process.

In this chapter we will review the meaning of concept learning, and how it can evolve to include videogames as tools that support pedagogic development. We will offer a vision of games as didactic tools and of how they should be used as instruments in the field of Special Education using *Multiple Intelligences Theory*. We will introduce Sc@ut DS, our new tool for learning communication concepts direct at autistic children. Section 4 presents an example of our ideas, a videogame to learn the vowels using some rules that could be followed to develop didactic units, on games using the *Stimulus Equivalence Theory*. Finally, Section 6 outlines our conclusions and future lines of work.

5.2 Learning by Playing, Playing to Learn: Videogames in Special Education

Can people learn by playing? This is a question largely debated by specialists in Psychology and Pedagogy. Before answering this question, we should understand the meaning of Learning and Playing and whether these concepts can be combined to create new applied learning methods without forgetting that we are working in Special Education. Therefore, we ought to adapt the contents to the characteristics and restrictions of these groups.

Learning can be defined as the form of acquiring knowledge by studying and gaining experience. The learning process involves being able to associate semantic or mental ideas with real world objects, establishing a relationship between the mental world and the real one.

Sometimes, traditional learning mechanisms make students loose interest in the subjects. Both the studies and the lack of interest often make the learning process stressful.

In *Special Education* the learning process is usually limited to cognitive weaknesses. It is essential to relieve students of the pressure exercised by traditional techniques and to look for new mechanisms that would help to increase both attention and motivation levels and to assimilate new concepts.

We can define *playing* as the action or set of actions directed at having fun or merely at spending time. When playing, we follow a series of rules to solve a problem individually, or collaboratively, against other players or a machine. A video game is a computer program specifically created to entertain. It is based on the interaction between a person and a machine. Here is where the video game starts to run. These programs recreate virtual environments where players can mainly control characters or any other element to accomplish one or several goals by abiding a set of rules.

The video game industry is currently collecting, in terms of turnovers, about €1.454 million in 2007 only in Spain – Data published by ADeSe (Spanish

Distributor's Association and Software's Entertainment Editors). Many specialist educators agree on the importance of video games in the present social context [2].

In the scholar context, video games have been traditionally considered as simple entertainment mechanisms to be used out of classrooms, thus missing their advantages as learning tools: scholar success, cognitive abilities development, motivation, attention and concentration [3].

Videogames have important advantages as learning tools, but they have serious negative effects when the players play them excessively in a non-controlled way, like aggressiveness, gender prejudice and immersive effects [4].

After introducing some concepts about the learning process and their application in classrooms, we wonder whether it is possible to apply them to Special Education too. When playing, we can create situations where we can examine our own limits in a self-regulated way. The game is the mediator of the learning process. But the use of video games in Special Education has shown significant problems:

1. Educational video games are often not designed for people with special needs. Few video games with educational content may be used in this context.
2. The already existing video games for special education are mainly didactic units which have lost the essence and attributes of games.
3. The devices onto which these didactic games are installed on are just simple PCs. They often do not raise children's interest.

Due to the above mentioned reasons, it is necessary to act carefully when transferring the experiences of games in the field of General Education to the area of Special Education. New design mechanisms must be proposed to develop these kinds of games. This should enable people to overcome their cognitive deficiencies and to increase their social integration level by applying the suitable techniques during the design of these games.

In order to favor accessibility in Special Education we have used Gardner's *"Multiple Intelligences" Theory* [5]. This theory states that Intelligence is not a unitary and indivisible concept but a set of abilities or capabilities that can be trained (Fig. 5.1). Video games can be very useful mechanisms to enhance different abilities. It is possible to use *other intelligences* to improve another *weaker intelligence* by creating worlds and situations that allow a child to act upon a subset of abilities to surpass the problems associated to others.

Our didactical videogames proposal starts from this main idea: The principal child activity must be *playing*; the consequence of this action (playing) will be that the child *learns* the educative contents in an implicit way.

5.2.1 Videogame Design Guidelines for Special Education

In the videogame design process, we should use videogame concepts already commented in previous sections to obtain the most successful videogame possible. It

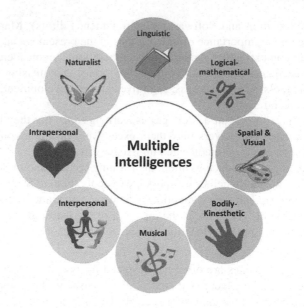

Fig. 5.1 Multiple intelligences and their relationships

is essential to improve *motivation*, *attention*, *concentration*, and *emotion* when the player plays the game [6–9].

In the design Process, the first step is to create a complete *Storyline* that must be attractive to the future player. A good story offers "good connection" between game and player and helps to catch the player's attention. Consequently, the story creates crucial motivation mechanisms that guarantee the interest of the child in wanting to play the game [10]. In this way, it is guaranteed that, if the child enjoys the educational contents, he/she will assimilate them in a relaxed way, because the principal action is to play and not to learn – learning is a consequence of playing. The story should *motivate*, excite and thrill the child/player [2].

The next step is the *Gameplay Design*. It includes all player experiences during interaction (what the player can do and how to do it) with the game. For example, goals, rules, learning curve, etc. This term is used to describe the overall experience of playing the game excluding the aspects of graphics, sounds, and the storyline. In *Gameplay Design*, there are some exceptional points for "special" players and their cognitive skills.

The game must offer *Feedback* for each action. This feedback is focused on the cognitive concept that the child must train when playing. To develop this feedback we will use different game interaction methods as supporting tools and also the child's profile. It is important not to create frustration in our players due to their mistakes. Errors should be corrected without causing sadness or discouragement.

It is recommendable to use a main character or hero, who acts as a guide in the learning process and game. Children should see themselves reflected in this hero. The hero is the mediator in the learning process and the one who carries out the actions; the hero must be very expressive and help to obtain positive action assimilation.

Each game must have goals. The learning process should be gradual, based on multi-levels or missions where the difficulty level increases gradually. At each level the cognitive weakness should decrease. To give rewards for correct actions: animations, songs, videos, points, objects, and even, gifts in the real world. Rewards offer an extra motivation–satisfaction factor; they allow us to create mechanisms that influence the player's self-improvement and advancement while playing.

With this design guide we could create a videogame without forgetting the objectives that we define in a videogame as learning tools: *entertainment, motivation and enthusiasm of overcoming*.

5.2.2 Didactical Contents Design Guidelines

When we are designing an educational videogame, we should focus on a set of points that determine if our game, as a videogame, will be a success and model the *Didactic Unit* into the game. We need to identify the *Player's Profile*, his/her limitations and cognitive capabilities in order to choose the best game and user interface mechanisms. We have to develop the adaptive mechanisms to help the player solve the educational challenges, structure and adapt the Didactic Unit to the player's characteristics and the game goals. It is important to reach a balance between what we want to teach and what should be learned.

The *Educational Contents* should be introduced into the game structure in a hidden way. The game should have its objectives as a game, and special objectives as a learning tool. Hence, the child can learn indirectly while playing.

According to the Videogame Design Guideline we start defining a specific *Didactic Unit*. It is integrated inside the *Game World*. Every *Phase* of this world has one *Conceptual Content*. In every level of this phase, we train the conceptual contents with the *Procedural Content*. We can use different activities to practice these didactic contents with the videogame challenges.

5.3 Sc@ut DS: Playing for Communicative Learning

As an introductory example of video games as special education tools, we have developed Sc@ut DS [11]. This project is an evolution of another project called Sc@ut and is an alternative and augmentative communicator (AAC), developed by the research group GEDES of the University of Granada using PDA devices as hardware platforms.

We have observed a series of deficiencies in PDAs during the use of this communicator: *Fragility*, the touch screen is very delicate, getting scratched or breaking easily, *Battery Life*, about 3 hours, *Multimedia*, the main memory is limited and consequently also multimedia objects and user interfaces which make them unattractive to children and *Price*.

The main goal of this project was to obtain a new attractive and a less limited platform than Pocket PCs for children and to change the communicator's philosophy to
develop a learning tool using game concepts. To develop the new communicator we
have selected Nintendo DS^{TM} instead of other alternatives such as PSP^{TM} (Playsta-
tion Portable) or UMPCs (Ultra Mobile PCs), because it has two screens, one of
them is a touch screen which offers more interaction possibilities, great multimedia
options without apparent limitations of memory, connectivity (Wi-Fi with other DSs
and PCs) and they are designed to be used by children.

The main didactic goal is to increase interaction and social communication. Children learn how to make sentences to express their desires and feelings. The device
makes the learning process easier by imitation.

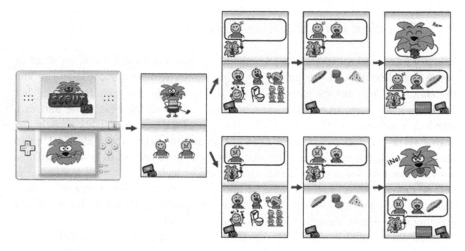

Fig. 5.2 Cause and Effect represented jointly on Sc@ut DS

We use both screens to show a suitable feedback, using videos and animations
without losing the context of the action, and to show jointly the cause and the effect
of the action (Fig. 5.2). Concepts are represented by pictograms whose designs
are personalized according to the ideas of the personal world of each child. In
order to improve the grammatical language in communication, we show the syntactic path to be followed. In this way, children can learn how to communicate
using a simple structure of pictograms which represent the mental idea they want
to express.

We have created a series of animations. Thus, children can correlate the grammatical structure with the mental idea in an entertaining way, and finally they can
associate it with the correspondent action in the real world.

The device reproduces an audio file that expresses the concept selected by the
child. When he/she finishes a sentence Sc@ut DS shows the complete pictogram
path and reproduces the full oral phrase. Our hero is "Leoncio, The Lion". He is the
mediator in the learning process and the one who carries out the actions following
the pictograms' path.

5.4 Practical Examples of Didactical Videogames

When didactic games for special education are developed, psychological techniques must be used to help overcome the user's cognitive limitations. In our situation these limitations are autism and cerebral palsy. We apply Sidman's theories about "Equivalent Relationship" and more explicitly the "Stimulus Equivalence" mechanism [12].

Our goal is that children learn how to associate letters, words or sentences to concepts. These concepts could be pictograms or videos that represent the action, with the correspondent oral pronunciation. A goal is to correlate food pictograms with the written word with direct stimulus training. On the other hand, indirectly, when a child listens to the oral pronunciation of the concept (pictogram), he could implicitly associate this sound with the written word by "Stimulus Equivalence."

As an example of videogames using the ideas that we have presented in this chapter, we will introduce our prototype of didactic videogame applied to special education: "Leoncio and the Lost Vowels Island" on Nintendo DS™ [13]. The main educational objective is to learn the vowels. The game is based on the learning method of reading/writing called "SuperLecto-Escritura" [14]. When the child responds correctly (he/she correlates pictogram with pictogram, later pictogram with vowel and finally with audio), the game shows appropriate feedback and emphasizes the pictogram and audio with the vowel. If the child fails, the game emphasizes the right answer and encourages the child to re-select a new answer. If the process of selection is right, in the following level of the vowel-phase, the pictogram will decrease its clarity, appearing the letter, which is "hidden" behind the pictogram. At the end the child correlates only the vowel with the pictogram. If the process and assimilation have been right at the end of the phase, the child will be able to associate a pictogram with the vowel, thanks to direct training and implicitly the child acquires the concept of vowel phoneme and completes the triple association pictogram-vowel-phoneme, the basis of reading/writing learning. An example of a game level is represented in Fig. 5.3.

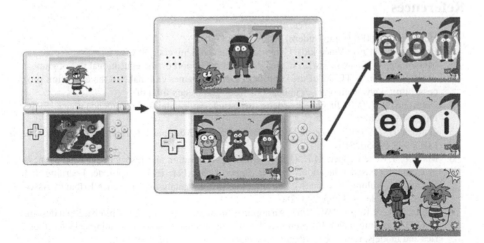

Fig. 5.3   Example Level in "Leoncio and the Lost Vowels Island" on Nintendo DS™

5.5 Conclusions and Future Works

In this chapter we have shown our studies using video games as a learning tool in special education. We propose a series of guidelines to design special education games and use video consoles as alternative devices since they are specifically designed for playing, as well being entertaining for children and offer better human–computer interaction adapted to certain collectives with disabilities. Examples of these premises and methodologies in this work have been in our videogames.

With the tests, we conclude that videogames in special education offer better spatial, temporal, and hand-view coordination ability, better concentration, motivation, attention, and reasoning capability, better assurance in the learning process and better assimilation of strategies and consequences in specific actions.

Children are happy playing and learning. This improves social relationships with other children and the environment in which they learn.

A future goal is to generalize the development process we are following and propose a complete methodology to create and design adaptative and personalized games based on playability techniques and users profiles in order to help in the social integration and the learning process of people with disabilities such as autism. We are currently developing new didactic games for other special education disciplines and the introduction of new alternative learning methods such as sign languages for deaf-mute or autistic children. We are working on defining playability attributes and properties/qualities and using them in the videogame software development to obtain more fun and playable videogames to play alone or with company.

In coming months, we will begin an experiment, with a group of children to check the efficacy of our videogames in "special schools" and elementary schools.

Acknowledgments This study and work is financed by the Consejería de Educación (Education Department) de la Junta de Andalucía (of the Council of Andalusia) as a part of SC@UT Project and the F.P.U Programme of the Ministry of Education and Science, Spain.

References

1. Huzinga, J. (2000) Homo Ludens. Ed. Alianza
2. Provenzo, E. (1991) Video kids. Cambridge: Harvard University Press
3. McFarlane, A., Sparrowhawk, A., Heald, Y. (2002) Report on the educational use of games: An exploration by TEEM of the contribution which games can make to the education process. http://www.teem.org.uk/publications/teem gamesined full.pdf
4. Cesarone, B. (2000) Juegos de videos: Investigación, puntajes y recomendaciones. ERIC Digest ED446825.
5. Gardner H. (1993) Frames of Mind: The Theory of Multiple Intelligences. Basic Books. ISBN 978-0465025107
6. Malone, T.W. & Lepper, M.R. (1987) "Intrinsic Motivation and Instructional Effectiveness in Computer-based Education." In R.E. Snow & M.J.Farr (Eds.) Aptitude, Learning and Instruction. Volume 2: Conative and affective process analyses. Lawrence Erlbaum Associates, Hillsdale, N. J., pp. 243–286.
7. Keller, J.M., & Kopp, T.W. (1987) An application of the ARCS model of motivational design. In C.M. Regeluth (eds.), Instructional theories in action: Lessons illustrating selected theories and models. Lawrence Erlbaum Associates, New York, pp. 289–320.

8. Csíkszentmihályi, M. (1990) Flow: The Psychology of Optimal Experience. Harper and Row, New York
9. Norman, D. A., (2004) Emotional Design: Why We Love (or Hate) Everyday Things. Basic Books, New York
10. Glassner, A. (2004) Interactive Storytelling: Techniques for 21st Century Fiction. Ed. Ak Peters.
11. González Sánchez, J. L., Cabrera, M. and Gutiérrez, F. L. (2007) Using Videogames in Special Education" R. Moreno-Díaz et al. (eds.), EUROCAST-2007, Springer-Verlag Berlin Heidelberg, LNCS 4739. pp. 360–367.
12. Sidman, M. (1971) Reading and auditory-visual equivalente. Jounal of Speech and Hearing Research, 14, pp. 5–13
13. González Sánchez, J. L., Cabrera, M., Gutiérrez, F. L. (2007) Diseño de Videojuegos aplicados a la Educación Especial. VIII Congreso Internacional de Interacción Persona-Ordenador (INTERACCION-2007. pp. 35–45
14. García, C. V., Luciano, M. C. (1997) SuperLecto-Escritura. Programa para el aprendizaje de la Lectura y Escritura. Ediciones Némesis, S. L. ISBN: 84-922930-8-X

Chapter 6
The InterMod Methodology: An Interface Engineering Process Linked with Software Engineering Stages

Begoña Losada, Maite Urretavizcaya, and Isabel Fernández-Castro

Abstract   InterMod is an interactive application design methodology which proposes using user-centred models to define requirements, describe human–computer dialogue, and evaluate prototypes. In addition, it promotes the early integration of interface models with system functionality. Based on Intermediate Description Design (IDD), which retrieves the formal description of models, InterMod makes it possible to quickly produce incremental prototypes and automatically adapt the design according to the modifications prompted by the evaluations.

InterMod is composed of a series of phases. In this chapter we will discuss performance order, the formal models in each phase and the relationship between them. The T-InterMod tool helps designers in the development process according to the steps proposed by InterMod. This tool translates the models to XML.

6.1 Introduction

In using interactive applications, it is common for the user to feel that their defined functions are difficult to understand or differ from his/her usual behavior. This problem is due to the fact that techniques for programming functionality have traditionally taken precedence over human–computer interaction techniques. It is important to note that the concept of usability [9] encompasses not only the efficiency and satisfaction of an interaction but also the effectiveness of a user's actions. Thus it is necessary to join both technologies: the design of usable interactive systems using user-centred methodologies and the practices of traditional software engineering. Numerous efforts have been made toward achieving this goal, as will be seen in Section 6.3.

B. Losada (✉)
Department of Computer Languages and Systems, University of the Basque Country U.P.V./E.H.U., Spain
e-mail: b.losada@ehu.es

J.A. Macías et al. (eds.), *New Trends on Human–Computer Interaction*,
DOI 10.1007/978-1-84882-352-5_6, © Springer-Verlag London Limited 2009

Among interface development methodologies, those which involve the user in the whole design life cycle [31], grouped under the name of user-centred methodologies, have dominated for some time. The InterMod methodology falls into this group; besides, it includes early functionality validation with the user by means of typical human–computer engineering techniques.

In order to address these questions, the rest of the chapter is structured as follows. The second section discusses classic life cycles in software engineering and user-centred models in interface development. The third section explains the different approaches some methodological proposals have taken for dealing with integrating software engineering with interface engineering. Next, we describe the outline proposed by the InterMod methodology. After that we describe the T-InterMod tool, which facilitates and guides InterMod performance, along with its modules and connections. We end with a few conclusions about our contribution to the development of user interfaces.

6.2 Software Development Life Cycles

A life cycle model shows the major phases and tasks of a software project, from its conception to its completion. In this section we begin by describing the classic models of software development, and follow up with user-centred models that have traditionally been suggested for interface development.

6.2.1 Traditional Life Cycles

In the field of software engineering, many attempts to find the optimal model for software development have been made.

The classic life cycle in software engineering is the waterfall model, in which tasks are sequentially connected and each phase is completely finished before the next is begun [28]. At the end, the components are tested to verify their correct functioning according to criteria determined in previous stages. However, Stone [31] showed that in practice the phases of development overlap and transmit information to each other. During design, problems with requirements are identified; during coding, design problems are detected, etc. The software process is not simply a linear model but rather requires a sequence of iterations in the development line. This simple vision has been extended [29], adding forward and backward iterations between the different steps.

The spiral model [5] has four phases: planning, risk analysis, engineering and evaluation. A software project goes through these phases many times, in a spiral that increases in number of iterations and cost.

In response to the two models outlined above, rapid application development (RAD) emerged [17]. RAD is characterized by iterative development and the construction of incremental prototypes in order to achieve greater development speed.

The Rational Unified Process (RUP) [4] is an architecture-centred life cycle approach especially well adapted to Unified Modelling Language (UML). The process, including user interface design, is guided by the use cases. Each phase of the RUP can be broken into iterations, and the software moves into the user community only in the last iterations, during the transition phase.

Agile software development [2] establishes the working software units as the measure of progress, and values both direct communication among team members over written models and the ability to quickly adapt to any changes over the development process planning.

Although the above approaches are commonly used in software development, their deficiencies tend to be associated with usability [7].

6.2.2 User-Centred Design

In ISO 13407 page 7 [11] we find user-centred design principles which include the following: *active involvement of users, appropriate allocation of functions to the user and the system, iteration of design solutions* and *multidisciplinary design teams.*

Unlike the traditional application-centred life cycle, user-centred design takes the user, his work and his environment as the starting point and designs and develops technology to support them [25]. Moreover, user-centred design is characterized by a rapid and iterative design process with continual evaluation.

As an example of the evolution of classic life cycles in the development of user-centred interfaces, Greenberg [9] (Fig. 6.1) proposes an iterative process for interface design and evaluation.

The star life cycle [10] (Fig. 6.2) takes evaluation as the centre point for all stages, as all aspects of the system are subject to continual evaluation by users and experts. The process is totally iterative; the development of the system can start at any phase and any other can follow. As a consequence, the requirements, design and product continually evolve until a definitive document is reached.

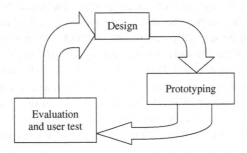

Fig. 6.1 Greenberg's process

Dynamic Systems Development Method (DSDM) [30] is a framework that follows principles of the agile methods. However, it also involves the user in its iterative

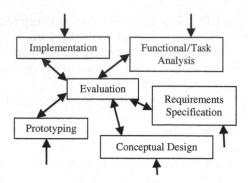

Fig. 6.2 Star life cycle

and incremental development. The process ends with a final phase in which the client is presented with an operational solution.

Agile methods differ from predictive software development processes as they provide a dynamic adaptation to the news contexts arising during the project execution. This emphasis on continuously improving and adding functionality throughout the project life, and the need of delivering pieces of working software, could derive on neglecting an organized development of the interface. Hence, solving these issues becomes a main purpose in the InterMod methodology.

6.3 Integrating Software Engineering with Interface Engineering

Software development is considered *engineering* in the sense that it must be realized by means of the structured application of scientific techniques. In the same way, developing user interfaces becomes *engineering* when techniques specific to engineering are used to create a product. It is precisely the use of these techniques upon which the quality of an interactive software product is based [8, 15, 20, 25, 26]. Both software and interface engineering share the same goal: the systematic development of a software product that meets quality criteria. However, both disciplines view this goal through different lenses and therefore are quite different; even though their phases share the same name, they are very different.

Traditionally, user interface (UI) development is carried out after the design of the functional part has been completed. In these cases, aspects related to usability are usually considered to be of lesser importance and, in this sense, solutions that seek to reduce design emerge, automating interface generation. This is the main goal of the Model-Based User Interface Development Environments in their first generation.

The concept of software engineering, which has traditionally focused on the development process, has evolved to include a usability process in the life cycle [12], as has been observed in various articles [8]. Approaches that integrate object-orientation with interface engineering (IE) practices apply IE design techniques in the early phases of the design life cycle. That is, when the first visions regarding scope, content and functionality take shape in the analysis phase.

The use of Unified Modelling Language (UML) in software modeling is widespread, and numerous efforts have used it to realize typical IE techniques. Thus, we find authors who have proposed extending UML [22] to include task models. Others look for equivalence among UML's own diagrams, such as the use case and activity diagrams, and in IE models, such as user task models [18]. It is also common to look to increase the power of UML activity diagrams [24] in order to represent IE concepts such as task order or type.

Use cases diagrams [13] are the only UML diagrams that provide an overview of the system's performance in response to interaction with the user, and thus are the tool that is usually used to carry out task analysis. Design based on UML use cases provides a way to specify, through the models, system requirements, user behavior and system functionality. A common approach is to use the UML use case model in conjunction with the description of each case. However, this type of use case model does not provide enough information about the user or usability in order to be able to reliably design usable interactive systems [23].

Essential use cases [6] are a variant used in usage-centred design which allows for a link between the usage and its interface by tying the user interface design into the system's essential purpose. Likewise, these authors introduce the notion of structured essential use case as one that is described in a systematic way in order to be used in the UI design and integrated into the rest of the development process.

Another proposal for integration comes from scenario-based design, which uses written descriptions of a system's use. An advantage of this is comprehension by users and designers who collaborate in its modification [26]. Similarly, our methodology proposes the use of formal models and intuitive prototypes for this purpose.

6.4 The InterMod Methodology

InterMod[1] (Fig. 6.3) [16] is a methodology for designing interactive tools and which proposes the use of user-centred models to define requirements, describe human–computer dialogue and evaluate prototypes. This methodology is characterized by the inclusion of a strict performance order, by the movement of information created in the different phases to descriptive models and by a continuous evaluation process which drives the iterations in the process.

The performance order in InterMod allows information flow between modules, which are continually fed and updated by the flow in iterative steps.

The information flow is based on an Intermediate Description Design (IDD) of the models, which keeps the description generated in successive phases independent, both in the engineering models used and in the graphic design phase. IDD serves

---

[1] InterMod is the current evolution of the INTERGRAM methodology.

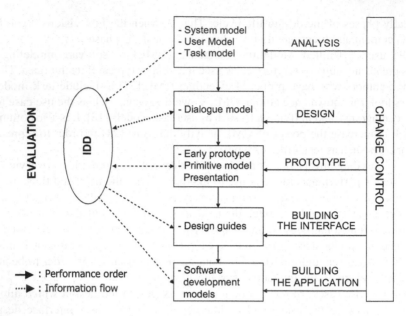

Fig. 6.3 InterMod Process

as a central storage point for the information, the arrival and departure point in each phase. It allows a completed product to be recovered and for modifications to be made to the original conception models. Additionally, it is possible to quickly produce incremental prototypes and automatically adapt the design according to the modifications prompted by the evaluations.

The process is embedded in a progressive evaluation discipline that guides the iterations. The iterations are not repetitions of the whole process, as occurs in the spiral model or in RUP, but rather the progressive evaluations condition changes in different phases of the project, which allows faster development. We distinguish between two types of evaluations: User evaluations carried out with prototypes through early prototyping techniques, and heuristic and metric evaluations carried out by the system according to criteria established in the system model and the user model.

In line with user-centred designs, our proposal insists on, like the star life cycle shown in Fig. 6.2, the integration of the evaluation process into all disciplines of the life cycle rather than just at the end, as occurs in the classic waterfall life cycle. Thus, we propose the same basic phases as traditional models, but we add prototyping and evaluation disciplines, like in the star life cycle. The software prototypes obtained and tested in different moments become the primary measure of progress, instead of the completely developed pieces of working software as it occurs in agile methods. Besides, we suggest organizing and developing the whole project by means of a task model.

6.4.1 Integrating the Software Engineering Process with Interface Engineering in InterMod

According to Mayhew [19], user requirements as well as the user interface design should guide the software development process, instead of being guided by or incidental to the development process.

We believe that both processes should work together. One aspect of this methodology that stands out is the inclusion of a system model that is linked to the user model in the analysis phase. This not only permits the realization of the dialogue model but also allows for the validation of the effectiveness of the functionality which will be extended in later phases in the software development process.

Figure 6.4 shows the process performance order. First, the user model, which gathers the properties, limitations and its performance method, is created. The task model, which describes user performance in fulfilling each task, follows from the user model. The system model collects the properties, limitations and system performance for each task completed by a user. The system model and the user model contain the information needed to complete the dialogue model.

Software development models are needed in order to implement the application's functionality; the dialogue model guides interface implementation and the system model is taken into account when the prototypes are evaluated.

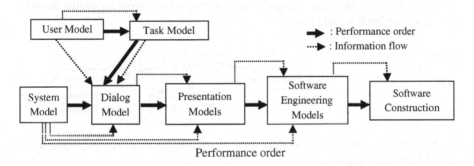

Fig. 6.4 Performance order

In the analysis discipline, the user model and the system model are included separately, each with clearly delineated purposes. In this way, the first evaluation with the user checks the coherence of a future scenario against the user's characteristics and performance. The second evaluation, carried out after the dialogue model has been completed, includes functionality and product navigation checks.

Separating user actions from system responses has already been suggested [32], and this alternative, used to integrate interface engineering and software engineering, differs from the employment of use cases in a series of practical tasks:

- User tasks and system actions are clearly separated. Evaluations are carried out with different techniques and with different goals.
- The system acts guide the flow of human–computer dialogue, whose navigation will facilitate the realization of interface prototypes.
- The information contained in the user model and the system model includes, in addition to the user and system actions, characteristics that allow the design to adjust to the user type as well as non-functional system requirements that should be taken into account and validated from the beginning.

6.5 T-InterMod Tool

A first demonstrator of the T-InterMod Tool (Fig. 6.5) has been built, and its main components are Diagram and ProtEval. It has been produced to validate the Inter-Mod methodology and facilitate its application. It follows a user-centred design (Section 6.2.2) and uses formal interface engineering techniques and models to carry out the processes described in InterMod. In addition, it generates documentation in User Interface Markup Language (UIML) [1] and continually updates it during product development, allowing the design to be modified and reused. This tool helps to produce well-evaluated designs and, in short, to develop usable applications. Moreover, the process helps the designer's task by allowing quality designs to be achieved on a sound basis.

Fig. 6.5 Outline of the
T-InterMod Tool

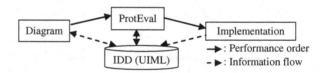

Diagram uses the formal models used by the designer to represent the user-scenario interaction form.

In order to represent repetitive or alternative/disjunctive tasks, we have chosen to combine HTA notation [3] with JSD notation (Jackson Structured Diagram) [14] in our applications to carry out task analysis. As a result of the process carried out by Diagram, interactive elements and their performance in navigation are already determined.

Currently, we are working to include the following aspects in T-InterMod:

- Evaluation of the user task model using participatory tools, where both the user and the designer decide on changes.
- Construction of the dialog model realized by means of including system actions in the task model.
- Heuristic checks of the navigation defined in the dialogue model, especially checks relating to user control and freedom.

ProtEval produces the interactive site's storyboard from earlier models, and automatically obtains software prototypes taken directly from the intermediate description generated by Diagram so that they can be evaluated by users. Two important phases stand out in this cycle:

1. *Prototyping phase*: Using techniques similar to paper-based prototyping [27], the different aspects related to the prototype's presentation model should be detailed.
2. *Evaluation phase*: Through feedback received from potentials users, the validity of the designed prototype is evaluated. In this phase, ProtEval is mainly centerd on the "Thinking Aloud" application technique [21], where the main idea is to obtain the user's opinion while using the system to avoid rationalizing at a later date.

6.6 Conclusions

InterMod is a simple and coherent user-centred model that allows the interface design to adjust to the user model. It proposes a performance order among phases that allows for the guidance of user performance as well as for the creation of evolving prototypes in order to minimize the iterations in the process.

It includes a system model in the analysis discipline, which allows early integration of software engineering and interface engineering. After realizing the dialogue model, successive prototypes will include the results of the system's functionality.

Currently, InterMod is being used in several businesses[2] and in academic applications at the university level.[3] The variety of applications that have been developed thus far have permitted us to check and refine the methodology, and therefore arriving at a useful proposal.

T-InterMod is an interface design tool that follows the process described in Inter-Mod, and the tool itself was developed using the methodology. It makes usable design easy, and adapts to the needs of users by using continual evaluation techniques. It also considers models and specific software engineering techniques for this purpose. The use of intermediate description in UIML contributes to independence and allows reusability.

Acknowledgments   This work has been supported by the Spanish Ministry of Education and Science, grant TIN2006-14968-C01; and by the University of the Basque Country UPV-EHU, grant EHU06/111.

---

[2]Master Thesis: "User Centered design for a production company web site" in SEAL S.A. Company.

[3]Subject: Human–Computer Interaction, in Computers Science Degree. University of Basque Country.

References

1. Abrams, M., UIML Specification, 2004, http://www.uiml.org/specs/index.htm
2. Agile. Manifiesto for Agile Software Development. Technical report, 2001 http://agilemanifesto.org/
3. Annett, J., Duncan, K.D. Task analysis and training design. Occupational Psychology, 41, (1967)
4. Booch, G., Rumbaugh, J. Jacobson, I. The Unified Software Development Process, Addison Wesley, 1999
5. Boehm, B. "A Spiral Model for Software Development and Enhancement", Computer, Vol. 21, no. 5, May 1988
6. Constantine, L. L., and Lockwood, L. A. D. Structure and style in use cases for user interface design. In Mark Van Harmelen (ed.) Object Modeling and User Interface Design: Designing Interactive Systems, 2001
7. Dix., A, Finlay, J., Abowd, G., Beale, R. Human–Computer Interaction. Prentice Hall, 2004
8. Ferre, X., Juristo, N., Moreno, A.M. "Improving Software Engineering Practice with HCI Aspects", Computer Science, Vol. 3026, pp. 349–363, 2004
9. Greenberg, S. Teaching human–computer interaction to programmers. Interactions, ACM-Press, vol.3, no. 4, 62–76, 1996
10. Hix, D., Hartson, H.R. Developing User Interfaces: Ensuring Usability Through Product and Process John Wiley and Sons, New York NY, 1993
11. ISO (International Organization for Standardisation), 13407, p. 7, Human-Centered Design Processes for Interactive Systems, 1997
12. ISO (International Organization for Standardisation), 12207: 1995/Amd. 1:2002 Information Technology. Software Life Cycle Processes. Amendment 1.
13. Jacobson, I., Christerson, M., Johnson, P., Övergaard, G. Object-Oriented Software Engineering: A Use Case Driven Approach. Reading, MA: Addison-Wesley, 1995
14. Jackson, M., "Principles of Program Design". Academic Press, 1975
15. Losada, B.; Lopistéguy, P.; Dagorret, P. "Etude de la Conception d'Applications Hypermédias" Congrès INFORSID'97, pp. 133–146, Toulouse 1997
16. Losada, B., López D., Martínez, J., 2007. Guía de actuación en el desarrollo de interfaces de usuario según la metodología centrada en el usuario INTERGRAM, VIII Congreso Internacional de Interacción Persona-Ordenador Interacción'07, Zaragoza.
17. Martin, J. Rapid Application Development, Macmillan Coll Div, ISBN 0-02-376775-8, 1991
18. Markopoulus, P., Marijnissen, P. UML as a representation for Interaction Design. OZCHI, pp. 240–249, 2000
19. Mayhew, D.J. The Usability Engineering Lifecycle. Morgan Kaufmann, 1999
20. Nielsen, J., Big paybacks from 'discount' usability engineering, IEEE Software 7, 3 (May), pp. 107–108, 1990
21. Nielsen, J. Usability Engineering AP Professional. Boston, MA, 1993
22. Nunes, N., Cunha, J.F. Towards a UML profile for interactive systems development: The wisdom approach. In Andy Evans, (ed.) Proceedings of the International Conference on the Unified Modeling Language, 2000
23. Nunes, N., Cunha, J.F. Wisdom-Whitewater Interactive System Development with Object Models. In Mark Van Harmelen (ed.) Object Modeling and user Interface Design. Designing Interactive Systems, p. 207, 2001
24. Pinheiro da Silva, P. Object Modelling of Interactive Systems: The UMLi Approach, 2002
25. Preece, J., Rogers, Y., Sharp H., Benyon D., Holland S., Carey T. Human–Computer Interaction, Addison-Wesley, 1994
26. Rosson, M.B., J.m. Carroll. Usability Engineering. Morgan Kaufmann Publishers, 2002
27. Snyder, C. Paper Prototyping: The Fast and Easy Way to Design and Refine User Interfaces. Morgan-Kaufmann, 2003
28. Sommerville, I. Software Engineering, 4th edn. Wokingham, England:Addison-Wesley, 1992

29. Sommerville, I. Software Engineering, 5th edn. Wokingham, England:Addison-Wesley, 1995
30. Stapleton, J. "Business Focused Development" 2nd. edn. DSDM Consortium, Addi-son-Wesley, 2002
31. Stone, D. C. Jarrett, M. Woodroffe, S. Minocha. User Interface Design and Evaluation. Morgan Kaufmann Publishers, 2005
32. Wirfs-Brock, R. Designing Scenarios: Making the Case for a Use Case Framework. Smalltalk Report, November–December, 1993.

Chapter 7
Designing more Usable Business Models into the RUP

William J. Giraldo, Manuel Ortega, Cesar A. Collazos, and Toni Granollers

Abstract A successful and usable interactive system requires cooperation between software engineering and human–computer interaction (HCI). But these disciplines consider user interfaces from different points of view. Therefore, interrelating activities into these two disciplines is complex. We propose to integrate activities related to usability into the business model. The Rational Unified Process (RUP) is a process aimed at complex projects and our view is that RUP is not a user-centerd method in itself. However, there is a possibility of enriching this process by taking into account the benefits of HCI. The main goal of this chapter is to describe a strategy that provides usability to the business modeling within the RUP.

7.1 Introduction

A successful and usable interactive system requires cooperation between software engineering and human–computer interaction (HCI). However these disciplines consider user interfaces from different points of view. Therefore, interrelating activities into these two disciplines is complex [1]. The system functionality is very difficult to reach if the integration of software subsystems does not consider the business model information [2]. The business model defines how real people interact between them and with resources to reach a common objective. Therefore, a business model should be human-oriented, permitting the understanding of the organization domain knowledge and its business [3]. It is called as problem domain model which should be independent of solution model.

The HCI area has become a field of great interest in systems that require high interaction with users [4]. There are many implemented systems that are not user centerd and, although they satisfy technical requirements and work correctly, they do not allow users to make use of all their capacities. The standard ISO-13407

W.J. Giraldo (✉)
Systems and Computer Engineering, University of Quindío, Quindío, Colombia
e-mail: wjgiraldo@uniquindio.edu.co

J.A. Macías et al. (eds.), *New Trends on Human–Computer Interaction*,
DOI 10.1007/978-1-84882-352-5_7, © Springer-Verlag London Limited 2009

provides some solutions to this kind of problem. These solutions must include multidisciplinary design, active users participation, distribution of functions, etc. [5]. The user-centerd design (UCD) refers to the process that focuses on the usability during the whole project development.

Business model has been not considered as an essential issue in the software development process. The first version of RUP did not contain a concrete approach in what concerns the specification of business systems [2].

Although RUP does not consider usability as a crucial aspect, through its ability to customize, there are proposals to provide it with usability [6]. This chapter considers some of these proposals into the business model (business architecture). We have studied a standard congress management system (CMS); this problem has been a common example in HCI literature where it has been always analyzed from the software perspective. The CMS offers services such as Register, Paper Evaluation, Paper Assignment, Paper Submission, etc. Although we have modelled this problem completely, we will present only two views of this model in order to illustrate the manner in which we have included the information of usability into Business Model.

Next section will describe related works, and then we will explain our proposal. A brief discussion will be depicted in the Section 4, and finally some conclusions and further work will be presented.

7.2 Related Works

Engineers dedicated to the software development have seen the necessity to have process models to apply them to the development of "their products" in the same way as it has been made in other engineering areas. As a result of these initiatives, several processes models, which have perfectly been documented in books and papers, have arisen [7]. Software Engineering is a discipline focused mainly on the functionality, efficiency and reliability of the system in execution. The current processes of development promote a fast prototypes generation of the software systems key requirements. Just as in the case of the software engineering, several authors have proposed valid process models for the design of user interface [1]. These proposals allow the developers to implement their applications under usability parameters. Some of these proposals are focused on the work of the heuristic evaluation [8], others on the contextual design [9], the essential use cases [10], the development of scenarios [11], etc. Granollers proposes the Model of Process of the Engineering of the Usability (MPIu+a) that is based both on the Software Engineering and on the HCI discipline following UCD approaches [7]. Ferre et al. [12] have related the activities into a user-centerd process with the common activities undertaken in a generic software development process, as it is understood from the software engineering perspective, so that software developers can understand this scheme. GÖransson et al. [13] add a new discipline called "Usability Design" to the RUP, in order to make this process more user centerd. Philips et al. [14] incorporate two artifacts that support prototyping and modeling of interfaces, creating a bridge between them. Anderson et al. [15] integrate usability techniques into RUP in a project in the medical area. They state that usability is necessary in order to improve user's satisfaction to obtain a better position in the market. Souza et al. [16] propose the adaptation of the RUP for having HCI aspects integrated into its main workflows; this adaptation is called RUPi. Lozano [17] propose IDEAS, which is an interface development framework. It studies the software engineering and usability gap.

As we can observe, there are some approximations in order to include usability aspects in the software development processes; however, they are not integrated in the business modeling. This research is important because it incorporates advances carried out in RUP up to now.

7.3 Our Proposal

A more effective form to organize the information of the users in the models of the RUP is proposed by using previous works. The suggested way is to improve the usability by capturing a more significant amount of useful information in the business model. In this chapter, a meta-model is presented to guide the best location of user information on the models. Some models of the case of study and the traceability between the RUP models are illustrated. The case of study is a Congress Management System. Although many researchers and developers agree on describing the RUP as a software developmental process, this one goes a step beyond the software specification permitting the specification of the whole organization [2]. The RUP uses the Unified Modelling Language (UML) applied for system engineering as well as business engineering [2]. HCI researchers have studied the UML applicability in HCI and they propose a good way to relate the two design spaces of HCI and software engineering by applying UML. "This could only be achieved by modifications such as: (1) extending the basic UML notations, (2) modifying existing notations, or (3) somehow linking the UML diagrams to separate external task models" [18]. The last version of RUP includes the business modeling discipline. Although it does not present a detailed business architecture, it defines some views to represent systems to be developed, such as [2] marketing view, business process view, organization view, human resources view, domain view, geographic view and communication view.

7.3.1 Business Architecture

The business architecture specified by RUP has a very high abstraction level. There are three differentiated levels: the business system, the software system and the technical system. Usability Engineering and user-centerd design normally begin their activities at software architecture level. However, useful user information available in business system should be captured. Butler states the users are involved in a conceptual model of three layers when they use interactive systems to support their work [19]. In the RUP, the software architecture is guided by 4+1 views. However, the same should be done in business modeling using Zachman's views [20]. Zachman specifies more complete and less abstract business architecture [21]. We propose to combine usability aspects in the RUP business architecture using Zachman's approach.

7.3.2 Business Modeling

The business model, a human being–oriented model, specifies the interactions between people and technology [3]. Therefore, it must include usability specifications. In particular, we must design for real humans who need software systems. The goal of business modeling is to define the strategy to provide value to the clients. Value-centerd HCI is an approach oriented to the value generation [22]. Gould et al. [23] suggest that developers should decide the users to be involved in the process in the first opportunity they have. The artifacts describing end users must be written only after substantial, firsthand contact with users [24]. The artifacts of the business modeling must be complemented as described in the next section.

7.3.2.1 Artifacts

Business vision: This includes people interacting with business, which can be either business workers or business actors. Business vision captures a description of the business's working environment and stakeholder characteristics, including their expertise, technical background, responsibilities, success criteria, deliverables, etc. [25]. The business vision artifact could be improved by the kinds of activities Gould describes [23]: observing users working, videotape users working, learning about work organization, and trying it yourself get users to think aloud while working.

Business goals: Business goals are mainly envisioned to obtain money. However, it is important to keep clearly defined user's goals. User's goals define business design mechanisms that are realized in the business process by scenarios. Business-oriented measures such as revenue and cost-perclick, to customer satisfaction-oriented metrics like page views, conversion and balk (or exit) rate could be appropriate for measuring success [26].

Business use case model: It describes the tasks (business use cases) that human business actors perform. It captures similarities and relationships between business actors by using generalization relationships [25]. Effective work allocation to business actors and workers in association with their responsibilities into the current process should be achieved.

Business actor/worker: Although not all of them become users of automated systems, an understanding of their characteristics provides a better understanding of the user environment [25]. Important usability relative information such as the social and physical environment, number of users represented, computer experience and social implications should be acquired.

Business analysis model: Business modeling discipline includes business analysis and design tasks. It captures the objects important to the domain and to users [25]. Within the RUP [24], a domain model should ensure consistency in all terminology and concepts of the user interface. Therefore, the design of the user interfaces and their abstract GUI (Graphical User Interface) components must be progressive and consistent with the evolution of this domain model.

Storyboard: Although Storyboard is not actually an artifact of business model [2], we propose it as a mechanism at the business level that should be captured early at any project. Business modeling artifacts specify activities and work products – independent of the technology – that can be realized by people. Each interaction between a person and a domain entity will require the specification of a prototype of its associate view. Storyboards are necessary to define the initial business scenarios. From storyboard we define initial prototypes of these views.

7.3.3 Arranging the Business Model

The relative information to the usability that is captured in the business model must be available in the design of the software system. In the software engineering, it is as necessary to raise the requirements as to control the traceability. Our proposal is to use a metamodel in order to not only locate the requirements but control the traceability in a more effective manner.

The metamodel proposed is based on Eriksson et al. [27] and RUP metamodel [2] (see Fig. 7.1). Examples of requirements are situations, problems, goals, business process, rules, etc. The metamodel describes how the goals are obtained from the problem domain. The problems are the difference between the real situations and states wished within the system, this is done by the stakeholders of the business. An example of this approach is presented by Remus et al. [26] by means of three scenarios of use on "Shopzilla," which is a comparison-shopping Web site. The metamodel illustrates relations such as process–activity diagram, actor–artifact, and activity–technology support. We are presenting two figures – Fig. 7.2 and Fig. 7.4 – where the arrows indicate the elements of the model associated to the relations mentioned before. They all contain user's information that must be captured with emphasis on usability.

Each business process is associated to an activity diagram which tries to group the subset of responsibilities – activities – associated to it. Every actor participating in the process is the owner of a group of activities – its responsibilities – instead of the activity diagram. This subset provides a definition of the context of use of possible software functionalities within an activity diagram (see Fig. 7.4).

Each business process is realized by a business use case realization (see Fig. 7.2). The realization specifies which business domain objects intervene in the execution of each business process. The domain object life cycle is modelled by a state machine. The state machine defines actions which could be related with actor interactions, such as creating, destroying or changing state actions. These actions may need software interfaces. In addition, the state machine makes possible

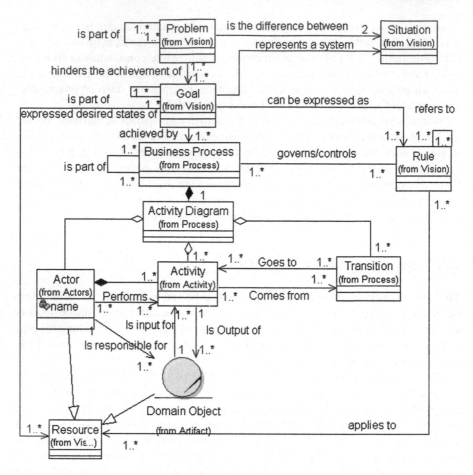

Fig. 7.1 Vision view of the business metamodel

the whole business processes coordination and it is a control mechanism of their internal interaction.

Prototypes should be used in elicitation of software requirements to capture scenarios and information related with usability. If either a business actor or a business worker requires technology support in order to execute his/her activities then he/she could be a software system actor. We should not forget that technology is not exclusively represented by the software system to be developed. It can be represented by any type of technological device. As a result, it is necessary to document this aspect thoroughly (see Fig. 7.3). At this point, functionality of software system is defined. It will require a set of interfaces for each user. It is important to remember that business workers or actors' realizations provide a very well-defined context for the specification of interaction between users and software. Butler [19] states that in order to improve the usability, the system's functionality should correspond

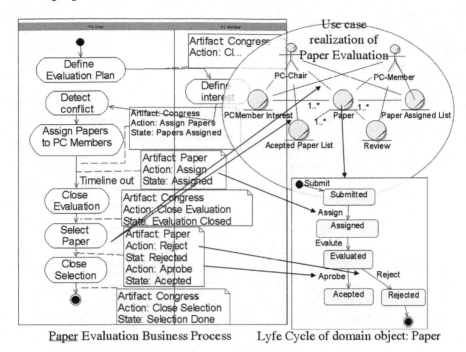

Paper Evaluation Business Process   Lyfe Cycle of domain object: Paper

Fig. 7.2 Business process "Paper Evaluation" of the case of study

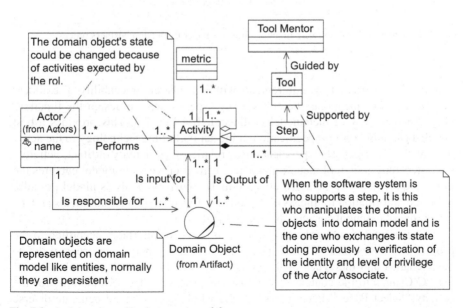

Fig. 7.3 Activity view of business metamodel

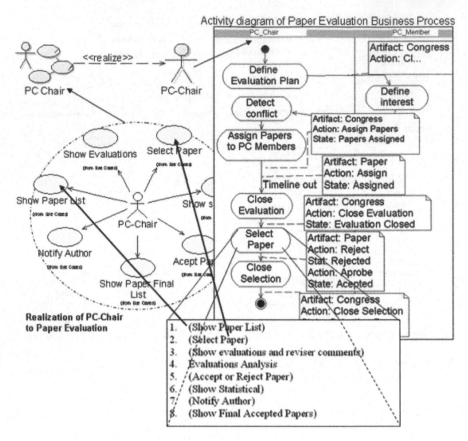

Fig. 7.4 Definition of the software functionalities for Paper Evaluation business process

clearly with the user's task requirements within a coherent traceability. The allocation of functions mentioned before is a key aspect when we design the functionality. Another view of metamodel is illustrated in Fig. 7.3. This provides a best detailed guideline for the specification of the support of the technology to the activities of the business. The specification of relationships activity–artifact, activity–step, step–tool, tool–tool mentor and actor–artifact in the meta-model captures the initial requirements of the software system. The business analysis model provides important information for the specification of software system requirements and the definitions of essential concepts in order to analyse it.

This is a vital point concerning the specification of interfaces according to the profiles and necessities of users. This aspect is also important in order to define the scenarios and dialogues of the system. Figure 7.4 illustrates a realization of the PC Chair into the context of the business process "Paper Evaluation" for the activity "Select Paper." Each activity in the whole system could generate diverse functionalities – use cases, see Fig. 7.4.

Each one is possibly generated in a different context. Consequently, the functionalities related to each actor are naturally different. However, shared functionalities can exist. This factor is very useful in order to define the interfaces of each actor. This traceability is achieved by identifying which automation points are inside the activity diagrams. The activity "Select Paper" contains seven steps, six of which are automated. They are represented into parentheses (see Fig. 7.4). Thus, we define the software system use cases associated to each system actor and its orchestration is defined in the activity diagrams.

7.4 Conclusions and Further Work

Nowadays there exist many and even better tools used to define user-centerd projects. This aspect is considered a benefit for the development team to reach objectives in what concerns quality, more specifically from the usability perspective. Comparing and personalizing methodologies are time-consuming tasks due to the amount of artifacts and activities that they provide. Consequently, it is necessary to consider different perspectives in order to cover a significant amount of these processes. The mentioned customizations are very useful for the specification of HCI. RUP reinforces the developmental process in order to transform it in a more effective tool in what concerns the product quality. One advantage of RUP is that it permits customizations by using the meta-model. The models of dialogue interaction are useful for modeling interfaces of different application services, mainly when the interface design is separated from the system design. A further study will be centerd in the customization of RUP that integrates the technique presented in this study. This technique will update RUP activities and artifacts. This customization must focus on the traceability that has to be developed concerning the creation of models that guarantee information consistence. This information should progress in each model in order to obtain an excellent isolation level in each architectural level. Finally, it is necessary to perform practical experiments to illustrate our ideas, which should be demonstrated in practice.

Acknowledgments This work has been supported by Universidad del Quindío, the Castilla-La Mancha University and the Junta de Comunidades de Castilla-La Mancha in the projects AULA-T (PBI08-0069), M-CUIDE (TC20080552) and mGUIDE (PBC08-0006-512), and Microsoft Research Project Fund, Grant R0308LAC001 and CICYT TIN2008-06596-C02-2.

References

1. Granollers, T., Lorés, J., Sendin, M., and Perdrix, F., "Integración de la IPO y la ingeniería del software: MPIu+a," presented at III Taller en Sistemas Hipermedia Colaborativos y Adaptativos, Granada España, 2005.
2. IBM_Rational, *Too Navigator (Rational Unified Process)*, 2003.
3. Couprie, D., Goodbrand, A., Li, B., and Zhu, D., "Soft Systems Methodology, A report," University of Calgary, 2004.
4. ACM and SIGCHI, "Curricula for Human-Computer Interaction," ACM Press, 2004.

5. ISO13407, "Human-centred design processes for interactive systems," 1999.
6. Kapor, M. "A Software Design Manifesto," *ACM Press*, 1996.
7. Granollers, T. "Mpiu+A. Una Metodología Que Integra La Ingeniería Del Software, La Inter-acción Personaordenador Y La Accesibilidad En El Contexto De Equipos De Desarrollo Multidisciplinares," in *Llenguatges i Sistemes Informátics*, vol. Doctorade. Lleida: Lleida, 2004, p. 511.
8. Nielsen, J. "Heuristic evaluation," in *Usability Inspection Methods*, J. Nielsen and R. L. Mack, Eds. New York: John Wiley & Sons, 1994.
9. Beyer H., and Holtzblatt, K., *Contextual Design: Defining Customer-Centered Systems*: Morgan Kaufmann Publishers Inc, 1998.
10. Constantine L. L., and Lockwood, L. A. D., *Software For Use: A Practical Guide to the Models and Methods of Usage-Centered Design*: Addison-Wesley, 1999.
11. Rosson M. B., and Carroll, J. M., *Usability Engineering: Scenario-Based Development of Human Computer Interaction*: Morgan Kaufmann, 2002.
12. Ferre, X., Juristo, N., and Moreno, A. M., "Improving Software Engineering Practice with HCI Aspects," presented at SERA, 2004.
13. Göransson, B., Lif, M., and Gulliksen, J., "Usability Design—Extending Rational Unified Process With A New Discipline," presented at Lecture Notes in Computer Science, 2003.
14. Phillips C., and Kemp, E., "In Support of User Interface Design in the Rational Unified Process," presented at Third Australasian User Interface Conference, 2002.
15. Anderson, J., Fleek, F., Garrity, K., and Drake, F., "Integrating Usability Techniques Into Software Development," presented at IEEE Computer, 2001.
16. Souza K. S., and Furtado, E., "RUPi -A Unified Process that Integrates Human-Computer Interaction and Software Engineering," presented at International Conference on Software Engineering–ICSE'2003, 2003.
17. Lozano, M. D., "Entorno Metodológico Orientado a Objetos para la Especificación y Desarrollo de Interfaces de Usuario," Thesis Doctoral, 2001.
18. Rourke, C., "Making UML the lingua Franca of usable system design," in *Interfaces Magazine from the British HCI Group*, 2002.
19. Butler, K. A., "Usability Engineering Turns 10," *Interactions, ACM*, 1996.
20. Ambler, S. W., Nalbone, J., and Vizdos, M., *Extending The RUP With The Zachman Framework*: Pearson Education, 2005.
21. Zachman, J. A., "A Framework For Information Systems Architecture," *IBM Ssystems Journal*, vol. 26, 1987.
22. Cockton, G., "Value-Centred HCI," in *Proceedings of the third Nordic conference on Human-computer interaction*: ACM Press, 2004.
23. Gould, J. D., Boies, S. J., Levy, S., Richards, J. T., and Schoonard, J., "1984 Olympic Message System: a test of behavioral principles of system design," presented at Communications of the ACM, 1988.
24. IBM_Rational, *Too Navigator (Rational Unified Process), Concepts: User-Centered Design*, 2003.
25. IBM_Rational, *Too Navigator (Rational Unified Process), Concepts: Usability Engineering*, 2003.
26. Remus J., and Frederick, J., "Million Dollar Web Usability Tips," in *Usability Interface*: STC UUX Community Newsletter, 2006.
27. Eriksson H.-E., and Penker, M., *Business Modeling with UML: Business Patterns at Work*: John Wiley & Sons, 2000.

Chapter 8
A Review of Notations for Conceptual Modeling of Groupware Systems

Ana I. Molina, Miguel A. Redondo, and Manuel Ortega

Abstract   The use of interactive applications to support group work is increasing. However, the development and, in particular, the design of this kind of applications is complicated. In recent years, the development based on conceptual modeling has acquired a greater importance and attention. This chapter presents a review of the main notations for the analysis and modeling of interaction and collaboration. This study has allowed us to detect that there are no proposals that tackle both issues jointly. We have created a methodological approach to solve this lack. This proposal includes notations, tools and procedures to give a comprehensive modeling support of groupware applications.

8.1 Introduction

The development of applications for supporting the realization of activities in-group is a difficult task due to, among other reasons, the multiple disciplines that come together in their design process. There are three main lines for the development of CSCW (*Computer Supported Cooperative Work*) systems: (a) the ad hoc development, in which systems are built completely tailored to the specific problem. This has been, up to now, the usual trend in developing of groupware systems. (b) The use of *toolkits* and APIs. Some useful APIs are JSDT, JMS and JXTA. Among the toolkits we find Habanero, Dream Team or Groupkit, and others. (c) The development of systems based on *CSCW components*, which allows the construction of CSCW systems by using predefined building blocks that can be reused and combined. Some examples of architectures and components are CocoWare .NET or Disciples, among others.

A.I. Molina (✉)
Laboratorio CHICO. Escuela Superior de Informática. Universidad de Castilla-La Mancha, Paseo de la Universidad, 4. 13071 – Ciudad Real, Spain
e-mail: AnaIsabel.Molina@uclm.es

J.A. Macías et al. (eds.), *New Trends on Human–Computer Interaction*,
DOI 10.1007/978-1-84882-352-5_8, © Springer-Verlag London Limited 2009

Another line of development is proposed in which the development process is based on *conceptual modeling of collaborative application*. This approach is in keeping with the model-based design, which is taking more importance in the field of user interfaces (UI) development. In this sense there are proposals for the conceptual modeling of interactive monouser applications that, however, do not provide modeling support of group work issues. We are interested in knowing and analyzing the existing alternatives for modeling both aspects (interaction and collaboration), in order to identify the main characteristics and/or lacks of such proposals. This analysis allows us to establish a set of requirements for the definition of a proposal which considers these both aspects (interaction and collaboration).

This chapter focuses on the development of a review of the main techniques that address the conceptual modeling of interactive groupware systems. In Section 8.3 a comparative study is presented. In Section 8.4 a brief description of the main features of our solution proposal is shown. Finally, we draw some conclusions extracted from this work.

8.2 Conceptual Modeling of Groupware Applications

In the research area of conceptual modeling of group work systems, there is not a suitable support of cooperative and collaborative behavior modeling, the use of shared spaces and communication technology. However, these issues become fundamental requirements to be considered during the development of CSCW applications. By reviewing Software Engineering (SE) and Human–Computer Interaction (HCI) literature, we can observe the existence of some notations proposed for conceptual modeling of group work issues. Among the more relevant contributions in the field of HCI we highlight the *ConcurTaskTrees* (CTT) notation created by Fabio Paternò [1], the *Group Task Analysis* (GTA) Framework [2], the CUA (Collaborative Usability Analysis) notation [3] and a task analysis method called MABTA (*Multiple Aspect Based Task Analysis*) [4]. In the fields of CSCW and workflow systems, we find the *Action Port Model* (APM) notation [5], which is taken as reference by notations such as RML, TaskMODL and DiaMODL proposed by Trætteberg [6] and the *Proclets* proposal [7]. As for approaches derived or completely framed within SE, we find two extensions of UML notation: COMO-UML [8] and UML-G [9]. We also consider the i* notation [10], which allows a goal-oriented modeling and is used in disciplines related to requirements engineering or organizational processes modeling.

Each of these notations presents a different way of approaching group work systems modeling. We are interested in their conceptual and methodological issues; that is, whether or not these notations are set in a methodological framework, as well as whether or not they are supported by the definition of a conceptual framework (*ontology*) that allows the reduction of ambiguities and establishes a basis for the aforementioned notations. Also, we are interested in learning about their support for group work conceptual modeling, as well as pointing out whether these techniques distinguish between cooperation and collaboration in the terms pointed out in Dillenbourg et al. [11]. In addition, we are interested in knowing which ones contemplate modeling interactive aspects (usually based on the distinction between user and application tasks) and, especially, if they tackle automatic or semiautomatic User Interfaces generation or the derivation of some type of software architecture for supporting the application. We also analyze whether these proposals have a CASE tool for supporting them. Finally, for each, we are going to point out their leading contribution, which makes them stand out from the others (i.e. the contribution that we consider most remarkable with respect to the rest). In Tables 8.1 and 8.2 we present notations for the group work applications modeling that we consider the most representative and we highlight their main characteristics. In Table 8.1 we present and summarize general and fundamental features: approach, ontology definition, the methodology in which they are framed and their most outstanding contribution. In Table 8.2 issues mainly related with modeling are summarized.

8.2.1 Comparative Analysis

As a result of the comparative study of main contributions in the field of group work modeling, we extract the following conclusions regarding their *general characteristics*:

- In the context of the Human-Computer Interaction, modeling support is usually based on the extension of the existing notations, by means of the incorporation of three new concepts: (a) The use of a new kind of task in the models (the *cooperative task*), which is also divided into individual tasks, carried out by the different roles involved in the system. (b) The possibility of indicating which roles perform which tasks. (c) The separation into models: cooperative and individual models. In this last model, an interactive task tree is created for each role involved in the group work.
- As for the *models validation*, GTA includes the use of ontology to validate the consistency among the various models proposed for specifying the system. Both CTT and COMO-UML allow the transformation of the models created by using these notations into formal representations, such as LOTOS and Colored Petri Nets respectively. Using formal notations allows the created models to be simulated and validated.
- None of the studied approaches supports the distinction between *collaboration* and *cooperation*. In many contexts, these terms are often used as synonyms. Dillenbourg [11] clarifies the difference, subtle yet important, between these two concepts. *Cooperation* entails the division of work to be performed, so that each person is responsible for his or her portion of work. Members of the group pursue the same goals, but act independently in their own tasks, or perform the same task but in separate parts of the shared context. *Collaboration* entails the mutual commitment of the participants, as well as a coordinated effort to solve a problem. Collaboration is, therefore, a superior activity, in which, in addition

Table 8.1 General and fundamental features of notations for group work applications modeling

Notation	Approach	Ontology	Methodology	Leading contribution
CTT	• Group centred (cooperative model) • User centred (A model for each role)	No	No	– It is an improvement to a notation from the HCI field – Distinguishing between Cooperative and Individual Model (tasks of a role)
GTA	• Group Centred • User centered	Yes	Yes (DUTCH)	– Uses ontologies for models validation
CUA	• Group centred	No	No	– Identifies a set of *basic mechanics of collaboration.*
MABTA	• Group centred	No	Yes	– There are *several modeling levels*, in which several *contextual aspects* are considered.
	• User centred			– *Task classification* (coordination tasks, making decision tasks, etc.)
APM	• Process centred	No	No	– Resources Modeling with interaction between users – Interaction Modeling based on the *speech acts theory* – Using *templates* or construction blocks and clichés or *patterns*
RML, TaskMODL & DiaMODL	• Process centred • User centered	No	No	– It incorporates different languages for domain, tasks and dialog modeling – Patterns

Table 8.1 (continued)

Notation	Approach	Ontology	Methodology	Leading contribution
Proclets	• Process centred	No	No	– Process Instantiation – Models reuse (components) – It explicitly tackles interaction among *proclets*
COMO-UML	• Group centred	Yes; Defining a Conceptual Framework	Yes (AMENITIES)	– Suitable integration with Software Engineering issues (notation derived from UML)
UML-G	• User centred • Group centred	No	No	– Clear identification of requirements to be considered in the modeling of *groupware* systems (shared data). – Use of extension mechanisms of UML for modeling these requirements.
Notation i* y derived (GRL, TROPOS)	• Group centred (SD model) • User centred (SR model)	Yes	Yes (TROPOS is a methodology)	– It allows the clear and simple expression of the actors' goals and dependencies among them – Differentiation between internal and external intentional elements

Table 8.2 Specific issues related to notations for group work applications modeling

Notation	Interactive issues modeling	Group work issues modeling	Distinguish between collab./coop.	Modeling supporting tool	Support for code automatic generation
CTT	Yes, distinguishing between interaction and application tasks; as well as temporal relationship among them	Roles, Cooperative Tasks, Objects (not graphically expressed)	No (only cooperation modeling)	Yes (CTTE)	The application TERESA generates code for mono-user applications, but not multiuser
GTA	Yes, incorporating specifications in UAN notation	Roles, Objects, Agents, Events, Tasks	No (Only cooperation modeling)	Yes (EUTERPE)	No
CUA	Yes, individual tasks can be represented by using HTA notation.	Scenarios, Tasks, Task instantiations (Individual and collaborative instantiation), Actions	No	No	No
MABTA	Yes, in lower-level abstraction stages, the use of HTA notation is proposed.	Operation, Action, Activity, Aspect	No	No	No
APM	No	Processes, Actions, Resources (Actors, Tools or Information Objects), Ports, Flows	No	No	No

Table 8.2 (continued)

Notation	Interactive issues modeling	Group work issues modeling	Distinguish between collab./coop.	Modeling supporting tool	Support for code automatic generation
RML, TaskMODL & DiaMODL	Yes	Roles, Actors, Groups, Actions, Tasks, Objects, Tools, Events	No	Yes (Visio)	No, but transformation is almost immediate
Proclets	No	Process (*Plocets*), Channels, Messages (*performatives*), Ports, Naming Service, Actors, Tasks	No	No	No
COMO-UML	No	Roles, Cooperative Tasks, Interaction Protocols	No (Only cooperation modeling)	Yes (COMO-TOOL)	No
UML-G	No	Shared Data, Notifications, Actors, Roles, Shared Activities	No	Any tool that supports UML modeling (Rational Rose, UML Argo, etc.).	No
Notation i* and derived (GRL, TROPOS)	No	Actors (Agents, Roles), Dependencies, Goal, Task, Resource, Intentional Limits	No	Yes (OME)	No

to cooperating, the work members have to work together on common tasks and towards a common outcome. The obtained result moves through different states to reach a state of final results obtained by the group. In the final product, it is difficult to determine the contribution of each member of the group. The collaboration assumes that the various members work within an area of common representation. To take this distinction into account is interesting for us due to cooperation and collaboration implying different ways of understanding the division of tasks (which affects task modeling), the participation of the different roles in the development of these tasks (which affects the task and role modeling), and the product obtained as a result of this joint activity (which affects the data model). Furthermore, cooperation involves the inclusion of special coordination tasks at the end of the cooperative activity to enable the group to collect their individual contributions in the final product (group solution), as well as making decisions or agreements in this production process.

As for the *type of notation* used for the task analysis and modeling, most proposals share the following *characteristics*, which we consider requirements, that must be considered in a proposal aiming to tackle the modeling of interactive and group work aspects:

- *Task decomposition*: It is the usual way that human beings work: decomposing tasks into subtasks of lower difficulty. There are several methods based on this feature for structuring and managing the complexity of the specifications. The use of a representation in the tree form to express the decomposition of tasks into simpler tasks is common (examples can be found in notations such as HTA, CTT, the work modeling in GTA or the MABTA notation). This decomposition can be done in tree form or can be based on the creation of new models representing specifications of a lower level of abstraction, as it is the case in APM and COMO-UML notations.
- *Task flow specification*: This is another aspect present in most of the specification techniques for specifying working groups. The task flow allows to indicate the order of execution of the tasks performed by the work teams. The order of the tasks is represented in most notations using temporal operators.
- *Data modeling*: Although the modeling of objects is closest to the design and implementation of the final tool, a subset of these objects must be shown and/or manipulated by the User Interface, as well as modified by the tasks performed by the application. Data modeling is considered by GTA, APM, RML, COMO-UML and i* notation.

To these initial *characteristics*, we have to add those that are suitable for *specifying group work*. In this regard, we point out the following:

- *Modeling of the organization*: The current modeling techniques must include the characteristics of the user as a member of a group or organization. Their position within a group can be specified through their responsibilities (i.e. the played *role*), and within the organization by the position occupied in its hierarchy. Most existing notations do not provide the modeling of hierarchical relationships within a group. However, this kind of vertical relationship affects the work to be performed by an individual who may be assigned or delegated tasks. This dynamism may also be made horizontally between people who are at the same level in the hierarchy. The modeling of these dynamic aspects is very useful in specifying an organization that is as realistic as possible.

- *Differentiation between roles and actors*: Both terms represent different concepts whose definition must be made clear. A *role* is defined as the set of tasks or responsibilities to play by one or more actors. An *actor* is a subject, human or not, that interacts with the system and can play a role at any given time. With regard to the actors, we are mainly interested in knowing their characteristics (e.g., their skills in using computers, their specific skills in a particular area, their language, etc.). The actors do not necessarily need to be specific individuals; they may represent classes of individuals who share certain characteristics. The actors perform tasks but always in the form of a specific *role*.
- The adoption of a specific *role* by an actor can be due to assignment, delegation, mandate or any other situation involving the work context.
- The distinction between roles and actors implies the adoption of *user identification systems*, as well as *user interface adaptation* to support the tasks assigned to a particular role. Moreover, knowing the characteristics that define specific actors allows *certain features of the system to be adapted to their preferences and/or skills*.
- Some of the proposals dealing with the modeling of the dynamic aspects of a system add the concept of *event*, which may be triggered or take place without users having control over the initiation of these events.

As is outlined in Lacaze and Palanque [12] conceptual models must contemplate *modeling of time constraints*. The temporal information that should be taken into account when analyzing and modeling user tasks can be classified into two categories:

1. *Qualitative temporal information*: Most of the notations consider a qualitative approach with regard to time modeling. In most cases it is limited to specifying a partial order among the activities to be carried out by the system. The specification of temporal relationships is based on temporal operators, such as sequence, iteration, choice, etc.
2. *Quantitative temporal information*: This kind of information is related to delays, dates and durations. There are few notations that explicitly include modeling of quantitative temporal information.

As for the notations analyzed, CTT includes both kinds of temporal information. This notation includes a wide set of operators that provide qualitative temporal information. Furthermore, this notation also allows the specification of quantitative temporal information, although it is not expressed graphically. The editor of CTT models (the CTTE tool) allows properties associated with the tasks and related to their duration (minimum, maximum and average amount of time for the performance of a task) to be included.

With regard to these aspects it would be desirable to include both types of information in a proposal that addresses the modeling of group work. That is, a set of temporal operators for expressing order and, therefore, a way to specify the coordination between tasks (qualitative information) and also periods of time (quantitative information). In this second sense, we will consider the representation of periods of time, dates associated with flow between tasks and time constraints.

8.3 CIAM: A Methodological Proposal for Developing User Interface in Group Work Systems

The review of these modeling techniques allows us to detect that there are weaknesses in terms of the modeling of collaborative issues, as well as lack of proposals to combine aspects of group work and interactive aspects. Therefore, the current state of conceptual modeling of this kind of systems is characterized by the following constraints: (a) There are no notations that *jointly approach* interactive and group work issues. (b) Necessity of defining a systematic method to guide engineers in the process of creating user interfaces for CSCW applications. These problems bring to light the lack of a methodological framework that supports the design of the presentation layer of collaborative applications. We have proposed a methodological proposal called CIAM (*Collaborative Interactive Applications Methodology*) [13] which consists of a series of modeling stages assisting the designer from the analysis of the work context to the interactive task model. This model can serve as a gateway to a MBUID (*Model-Based User Interface Development*) that allows to obtain a final UI in an automatic or semiautomatic way. The proposal consists of five main stages that guide the designer to change his analysis perspective until reaching models closer to the specification of the final UI (Fig. 8.1). In each of these stages a set of specification techniques are used, preferably of graphical nature, called CIAN (*Collaborative Interactive Applications Notation*) [14].

Fig. 8.1 CIAM methodological proposal stages

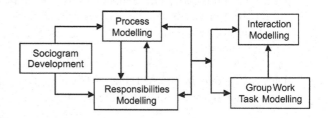

Comparing our proposal with other approaches in the same terms, which were analysed in Section 8.2.1 we can conclude that our proposal supports most of the features considered in Tables 8.1 and 8.2:

- CIAM can be considered a *mixed approach* that focuses on different modeling perspectives in several stages of the process. The first stages of CIAM tackle a more *group-centred* modeling, changing to a more *process-centred* modeling in subsequent stages to finally draw closer to a more *user-centred* perspective as we go deeper into the abstraction level.
- The creation of CIAN notation is based on a *metamodel* (ontology) [14]. This ontology served as a basis for the definition of the modeling techniques that are used in each of the stages of our methodological approach. It captures the concepts whose semantics is interesting to be represented by means of the group of views or modeling perspectives to be tackled during the different stages. This conceptual framework is composed by four *views* (or modeling perspectives): *organizational view*, *inter-action view*, *data view* and *interaction view*.
- We consider the most *outstanding contributions* of this proposal the fact that it *distinguishes* between *cooperative and collaborative tasks* and can *generate* the interaction model *from a shared context* definition.
- Unlike the rest of the studied approaches, CIAM considers *interactive* and *group work* issues jointly.
- In relation to the *modeling of group work aspects*, CIAN notation allows *group work processes* to be specified, being these group processes comprised of *cooperative, collaborative* and *individual* tasks performed by *roles* that manipulate *objects* and *shared data* to jointly reach the *objective* of the *organization*.
- As a result of the proposed process we obtain a set of CTT models that can be used as input in the existing approaches for *deriving a concrete and final user interface*.
- The CIAM methodology is supported by a *CASE tool* that allows editing and validating the models specified using CIAN notation. This tool is called CIAT (*Collaborative Interactive Application Tool*), and it supports the interface design of groupware applications, enabling integration with software processes through the mapping of models in CIAN notation onto UML models. The CIAT tool has been implemented by using EMF and GMF (*Graphical Editing Framework*). By using these technologies and the conceptual framework from which we created our methodological approach, we have created the CIAT tool as an Eclipse plug-in.

8.4 Conclusions

The development of groupware system is not a trivial task. If we want to base this process on a model-based design, we need a set of suitable specification artifacts. There are methods proposed within the SE, HCI, CSCW and *workflow* fields that are applied to model collaborative procedures. In this chapter, we have shown a comparative analysis of main notations from these areas. While reviewing these approaches, we have detected that there is no proposal that links interactive and collaborative issues. This has caused the development of a methodology that includes a set of notations, tools and procedures, called CIAM, which allows to solve this shortcoming. CIAM allows the UI design of groupware applications and provides a set of notations of graphical and textual nature (CIAN) with a wider capacity to represent all the diverse aspects to be considered in the design of groupware systems than the rest of the existing proposals. As a future work, we plan to improve the CIAM proposal with the aim of considering awareness mechanism.

Acknowledgments Work supported by the Castilla–La Mancha University and Junta de Comunidades de Castilla–La Mancha in the project mGUIDE (PBC08-0006-512) and M-CUIDE (TC20080552).

References

1. Paternò F (2004) ConcurTaskTrees: An Engineered Notation for Task Models. In: D. Diaper and N.A. Stanton (eds) The Handbook of Task Analysis for HCI. LEA, Mahwah, NJ., pp. 483–501.
2. van Welie, M. and G.C. van der Veer (2003) Groupware Task Analysis. In: E. Hollnagel (ed.) Handbook Of Cognitive Task Design, LEA., NJ. pp. 447–476.
3. Pinelle, D. (2004) Improving Groupware Design for Loosely Coupled Groups, in Department of Computer Science. PhD thesis, University of Saskatchewan.
4. Lim, Y.-k. (2004) Multiple aspect based task analysis (MABTA) for user requirements gathering in highly-contextualized interactive system design. Third Annual Conference on Task models and Diagrams (TAMODIA 2004). Prague, Czech Republic: ACM International Conference Proceeding Series.
5. Carlsen, S. (1998) Action port model: A mixed paradigm conceptual workflow modelling language. Third IFCIS International Conference on Cooperative Information Systems.
6. Trætteberg, H. (2002) Model-Based User Interface Design, in Department of Computer and Information Sciences. PhD. thesis, Norwegian University of Science and Technology.
7. van der Aalst, W.M.P., et al. (2001) Proclets: a framework for lightweight interacting workflow processes. Journal of Cooperative Information Systems, 10 (4): 443–482.
8. Garrido, J.L., Gea, M., and M.L. Rodríguez, (2005) Requirements Engineering in Cooperative Systems. Requirements Engineering for Sociotechnical Systems. IDEA GROUP, Inc.USA, 226–244.
9. Rubart, J. and P. Dawabi (2004) Shared Data modelling with UML-G. International Journal of Computer Applications in Technology, 19.
10. Yu, E. (1995) Modelling Strategic Relationships for Process Reengineering, PhD thesis, University of Toronto.
11. Dillenbourg, P., et al. (1995) The evolution of research on collaborative learning. In: P. Reimann, H. Spada, (eds) Learning in Humans and Machines: Towards an Interdisciplinary Learning Science. London, 189–211.
12. Lacaze, X. and P. Palangue (2004) Comprehensive handling of temporal issues in tasks models: What is needed and how to support it? In Workshop 'The Temporal Aspects of Work for HCI (CHI 2004)'. Vienna, Austria.
13. Molina, A.I., M.A. Redondo, and M. Ortega (2008). CIAM: A methodology for the development of groupware user interfaces. *Journal of Universal Computer Science. In press.*
14. Molina, A.I., M.A. Redondo, and M. Ortega (2006) A conceptual and methodological framework for modelling interactive groupware applications. 12th International Workshop on Groupware (CRIWG 2006). Valladolid, Spain: Springer-Verlag (LNCS), 413–420.

Chapter 9
Conceptual and Practical Framework for the Integration of Multimodal Interaction in 3D Worlds

Héctor Olmedo-Rodríguez, David Escudero-Mancebo, Valentín Cardeñoso-Payo, César González-Ferreras, and Arturo González-Escribano

Abstract This chapter describes a framework to integrate voice interaction in 3D worlds allowing users to manage VRML objects by using speech dialogs. We have defined a language named XMMVR to specify in a common program the 3D scenes and the multimodal interaction. XMMVR is based on the theater metaphor adding the possibility to include speech dialogs for the user to control the 3D action. This language is based on the XML standard reusing other standard languages such as VRML for graphics and VoiceXML for speech dialogs. We also describe a platform to support XMMVR that integrates the speech dialog manager, GUI interaction (graphical output and mouse input), task division, and event management.

9.1 Introduction

Virtual Reality Systems (VR) and Spoken Dialogue Systems (DS) strongly increase the potential of Human Computer Interaction (HCI) [1,2] adding complementary channels to the conventional input/output system based on a display and a keyboard or mouse. The integration of these researching fields can be seen as a natural evolution of both technologies allowing the navigation of VR worlds using the mouse and simultaneous object selection using speech [3,4]. Nevertheless the VR–DS integration has been hardly exploited in commercial systems despite of existing prototypes (see [5] for a review). The main reason for this situation is probably the youth of these work areas, where most efforts have focussed on improving separately both fields, instead of studying the necessities of interdependence derived from the combination of both. Here we present a proposal that combines VR and DS. We have also created a platform for developing applications based on 3D virtual worlds allowing multimodal interaction driven by spoken dialogue.

D. Escudero-Mancebo (✉)
ECA-SIMM Laboratory, Universidad de Valladolid. Campus Miguel Delibes s/n. 47014 Valladolid, Spain
e-mail: descuder@infor.uva.es

J.A. Macías et al. (eds.), *New Trends on Human–Computer Interaction*,
DOI 10.1007/978-1-84882-352-5_9, © Springer-Verlag London Limited 2009

Spoken dialogs can bring clear benefits to 3D virtual environments interaction: first because commands can be entered in hands free environments and second because users can refer to objects outside of the camera viewing. But there is a difficulty for general approximation to multimodal fusion that resides on the different natures of the metaphors each modality is based on. The three components of multimodal interaction in 3D environments are (1) three-dimensional model specifications of 3D objects in the virtual world, which can be static and/or dynamic; (2) graphical interaction (GUI) based on keyboard and mouse event model and on the action spaces metaphor [6] to organize three-dimensional user interfaces; and finally (3) vocal interaction (VUI) where four metaphors are possible: proxy, divinity, telekinesis or interface agent [7]. The combination of these three components in a common architecture will be influenced by the selected metaphor. The definition of a markup language to specify the three components (3D graphics, GUI interaction and VUI interaction) in a common framework is expected to make easy the development of a reusable architecture supporting these components and the programming of 3D stories based on the different metaphors mentioned above.

VR and DS are characterized by a relative availability of research prototypes and by some commercial system that generally has neglected the need of adjusting to any standard specification. VoiceXML [8] is the standard for DS. The standard for scene definition is X3D [9], an evolution of VRML [10]. These standards are a reference for developers to adapt their systems, with the consequent contribution to reusable modules portability. Our proposal is based on a markup language for the specification of 3D worlds with dialogue integration. The solution we contribute with gives argumental coherence to the definition of 3D scenes with spoken interaction by linking documents written in the available standards for VR and DS.

Several markup languages exist for specifying vocal interaction, scenes and behavior. VoiceXML, SALT [11], and X+V [12] are examples of markup languages for specifying vocal interaction. As markup languages for specifying scenes we have VRML and X3D. The limitations of these two languages for specifying the behavior of the integrated elements have caused the definition of markup languages for specifying behavior, as for example Behavior3D [13] or VHML [14]. As hybrid markup languages we can mention MIML [15] that allows the integration of speech and gesture information in the context of a given application. MPML-VR is an extension of MPML (Multimodal Presentation Markup Language), a markup language designed for multimodal presentations using VRML 2.0 to represent three-dimensional spaces through an anthropomorphic agent or human-like avatar [16]. Besides the mentioned markup languages, there are others focusing on specific applications [17]. None of the markup languages found in the state of the art has the goal of specifying virtual worlds with multimodal interaction. This goal is focused by the XMMVR, the alternative markup language that will be described in this chapter. This chapter first presents the XMMVR language. Next the architecture required to interpret XMMVR documents is described. We end with a comparison with other state of the art proposals, conclusions and future work.

9.2 XMMVR Language

The eXtensible markup language for MultiModal interaction with Virtual Reality worlds or XMMVR is a markup language to specify 3D scenes, behaviors and interaction. Each world is modeled by an XMMVR element, using the cinematographic movie metaphor. It is a hybrid markup language because it embeds other languages as VoiceXML or X+V for vocal interaction and X3D or VRML for describing the 3D scenes. The XML files that comply with the XMMVR DTD include links to the necessary programs and files needed to run the specified 3D world. Our system is event driven, so it is required to define a minimum list of events to substitute the time line.

Figure 9.1 shows the structure of an XMMVR document. Any *xmmvr* element is formed by a cast of *actors* named *cast* and a sequence of scenes named *sequence* determining the temporal evolution of the world. The element *context* is reserved for future use.

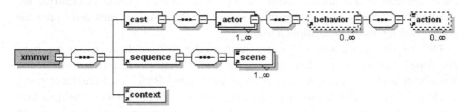

Fig. 9.1 Elements of the XMMVR language

The user is considered a member of the audience. He or she is able to interact with the actors of the world though is not considered as an actor of the world. Thus we use the *proxy metaphor* to specify the vocal interaction and the *theater metaphor* to specify the graphical interaction. The combination of both metaphors leads to a new metaphor that we call the *movie metaphor*.

Each *actor* of the cast is an element with graphical appearance described in a VRML file and a *behavior* that specifies the user interaction. Each behavior is defined as a pair *<event, list of actions>*. The actions are executed when a *condition* is met.

The user generates events using the graphical interaction *GUI* or the vocal interaction *VUI*. There are also system events to define the interaction with other actors of the world (*ACT* events) or to interact with the system (*SYS* events). The list of actions is a set of actions to be run when the event occurs. The actions can be of GUI, VUI, ACT, or SYS type. GUI actions modify the graphical appearance of the 3D World. VUI actions are dialogs. ACT actions are messages sent between actors. SYS actions are the navigation between scenes.

The *sequence* element schedules the *scenes* of the world. By defect the scenes are displayed in the same order as they are written in the document. SYS events and actions allow to navigate among scenes by changing the sequential default order. At least one scene must be defined in the xmmvr world. Interaction is only possible if at least one actor is defined.

According to these premises, a DTD [18] has been defined so that it is possible to develop multimodal applications by writing a XML file that complies with the XMMVR DTD. 3D scenes, actors, its behavior, and the interaction with the user are defined in the same markup file. This file is used by the system architecture to run the application as will be described next.

9.3 XMMVR Platform

We have created a framework to develop multimodal HCI applications where the flow of the interaction in 3D environments is driven by spoken dialogs. To build an application using our framework the developer has to specify the virtual world, the sequence of dialogues, and the list of actions to be triggered when the events are generated by the users. In the preceding section we described a language to specify these elements in a common XMMVR document. In this section we describe the architecture of the system responsible to parse XMMVR documents and to run the corresponding multimodal application.

One of our goals was to build a multimodal web application, so we have developed a system embedded in a web navigator. Dialogs are programmed using VoiceXML and 3D scenes, and actors are described in VRML. We have developed a world manager to schedule the actions to be performed in the 3D world using a Java applet. In the following sections we describe how the spoken interaction is carried out and how the system manages the overall 3D world behavior.

9.3.1 Speech Dialog Management

Figure 9.2 shows the components that manage the vocal interaction. There is a component embedded in the web browser, which starts the execution requesting a dialog to the *dispatcher*. It retrieves the corresponding VXML document from a *repository* and sends it to an *interpreter*. The VXML interpreter performs the dialog using the *voice platform*. The interface between the VXML interpreter and the voice platform are *prompts* (to be synthesized) and *field* (the output of the automatic speech recognizer) according to the VoiceXML standard.

We have developed the system using a Java applet on Internet Explorer web browser. It uses the VRML browser CORTONA [19] to show the state of the world. The GUI interaction is based on the EAI API [20]. We use a servlet in an Apache Tomcat server to feed the vocal browser of our dialogue system. We created our own VXML interpreter that uses the Ibervox ATLAS voice platform [21]. As the vocal components are distributed over different severs, multimodal applications can run in a conventional PC with audio and the appropriate browsers.

9.3.2 Management of the 3D World

The required components that make the 3D world react to events are shown in Fig. 9.3. The VUI events are dispatched by the *Spoken dialog manager* and the GUI

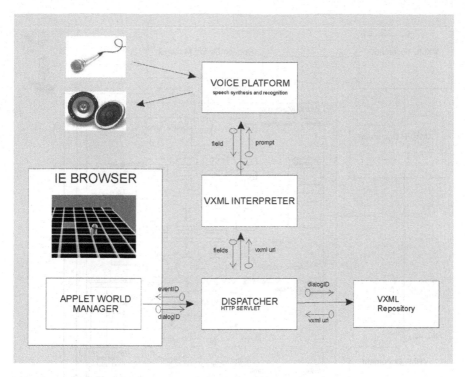

Fig. 9.2 Architectural components for the speech dialog management

events are typically generated by clicking the 3D elements. The system obtains the information about the 3D scenes and the actors from the XMMVR document. The same document specifies the behavior of the actors as pairs *<event, list of actions>* and links to the VRML document that specifies the 3D scene and actors. The left side of the Fig. 9.3 shows the relationship between two XMMVR actors named actor A and actor B and two 3D VRML elements named node A and node B. In response to the events, the system makes changes in the nodes, according to the specifications of the XMMVR document.

The first stage of the system is the *Event scheduling* task, where events are queued and multiplexed in a number of parallel queues (in this case four queues, but this parameter is programmable). Each queue is attended by the corresponding thread, and this allows the concurrent execution of actions in the scene. The threads access a hash table that contains the actions corresponding with the events, as described in the XMMVR document. If any of the actions is not elemental, the thread is responsible to decompose it, producing a new queue of elemental actions ready to be run by the *World manager* in the next stage. We have programmed an *Alarm manager* to enter anti-actions that eliminate several actions to be canceled when exceptional events occur (alarms).

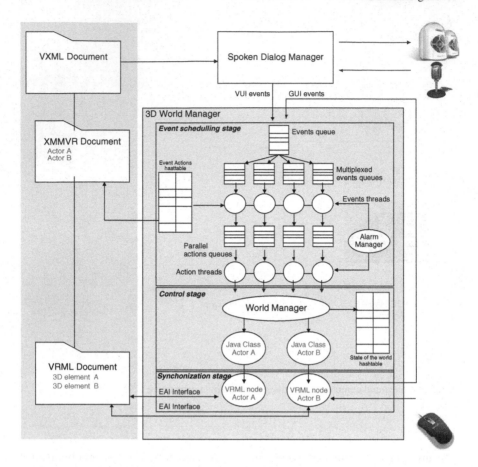

Fig. 9.3 Architectural components of the 3D world manager

Each 3D VRML element has two associated Java Classes: Control and Interface. Control executes elemental actions and interacts with the corresponding variables of the *State of the world hash table* and Interface manipulates the graphics of the 3D node. Between the Interface Java Class and the 3D nodes there is an interface (*synchronization stage* in Fig. 9.3) that is responsible to use the EAI to manipulate the VRML elements and to receive the GUI events and forward them to the system input. In the Fig. 9.3, the node A is manipulated through the Java Class Interface Actor A. The difference between the node A and the node B is that node B can potentially send GUI events such as a mouse click on the 3D VRML node B.

The *World Manager* reads the actions in elements and calls the corresponding Java Methods. Furthermore, it updates the *State of the world hash table* that stores the state of the properties of the world. The information of this hash table is used to assign values to the parameters of the Java methods. The manager is also responsible to update this table according to the executed actions.

9.4 Discussion

The W3C Multimodal Interaction Group (MMI) has recently defined the required components for a multimodal architecture and interfaces [22]. The *Runtime Framework* is the core of the architecture providing the basic structure and managing the *Constituents* communication (see Fig. 9.4). The *Delivery Context Component* of the framework provides information about the platform capabilities. The *Interaction Manager* coordinates the different modalities. The *Data Component* provides a common data model. The *Modality Components* offer specific interaction capacities. There is a straight projection of the XMMVR architecture onto this model: our Runtime Framework is a Java applet where the 3D World Manager is the Interaction Manager; the XML file complying the XMMVR DTD is used as the Runtime Framework markup; the VRML and VoiceXML files are used as the markup language for the graphical interaction/scene and vocal interaction Modality components; and the State of the world hash table plays the role of the Data component. The Delivery Context Component is to be implemented in future versions.

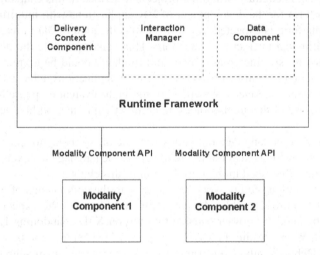

Fig. 9.4 W3C MMI constituents

Other related projects are COLLADA, MPML-VR, NICE, and CONTIGRA. The COLLADA project [23] defines an open standard XML Schema for exchanging digital assets among various graphics software applications. Our proposal aims to be not only an exchanging medium but a platform to specify scenes and behavior. XMMVR has similarities with the MPML-VR project mentioned in the introduction of the chapter. Indeed, the 3D avatar of MPML-VR is controlled on the base of transitions coming from *events* such as a mouse click or from *spoken input*, typically a voice command. We understand that XMMVR has a broader scope. NICE [24] is a project for developing interactive games where a scenario with characters is presented and the user can interact with the characters. Each character has a domain model corresponding to its vision of the world described in a tree-like representation that can be represented in XML format. The world is defined by scenes driven by dialog events that could generate java classes. CONTIGRA project [25] has defined Behavior3D to automatically generate XML Schemas building a repertory of the behaviors of a set of 3D widgets. The behavior description of the XMMVR language is inspired in Behavior3D.

9.5 Conclusions and Future Work

The definition of the XMMVR language shows that it is possible to write scripts to specify virtual worlds with multimodal interaction based on symbolic commands. The use of this language brings modularity, resulting on single development cycles and improving the possibilities to reuse or to standardize components. We have implemented an architecture supporting this language and we have illustrated its use with an example consisting on a 3D scene with two active nodes.

Our proposal, in contrast with other projects described in this chapter, is to build a generic platform for the development of VR applications with multimodal interaction. The platform is expected to allow the specification of 3D movies based on different multimodal interaction metaphors. This makes possible the development of applications for specific areas where multimodality could be a great support to ease the interaction in fields such as entertainment applications, educative games or handicapped people interfaces. We are working on the evaluation phase to value the benefits of the use of this methodology in contrast with other ad hoc development methods.

This version of the language only considers the proxy metaphor for vocal interaction. As future work, next versions are to extend the language to cover other interaction metaphors described in the introduction of this chapter.

Another challenging future work has to do with the components of architecture and the need to move to public domain tools and libraries. We expect to replace the Cortona by another browser capable to interpret X3D abandoning EAI API by SAI API [26]. We are testing FreeWRL [27] or XJ3D [28] that can be executed on platforms as Debian Linux. Concerning the vocal browsers, open source solutions are still difficult to find in nowadays state of art.

Acknowledgment This work has been partially financed by the research project of the Junta de Castilla y León VA077A08.

References

1. Sherman, W.R., Craig, A., *Understanding Virtual Reality: Interface, Application, and Design*, The Morgan Kaufmann Series in Computer Graphics, 2002
2. Dahl, D. *Practical Spoken Dialog Systems (Text, Speech and Language Technology)*, Springer, 2004
3. Bolt, R.A., *"Put-That-There": Voice and Gesture at the Graphics Interface* ACM Siggraph Computer Graphics, 1980

4. Cohen, P., Oviatt, S., *The Role of Voice Input for Human-Machine Communication* Proceedings of the National Academy of Sciences, 1994
5. González-Ferreras, C., González Escribano, A., Escudero Mancebo, D., V. Cardeñoso Payo. *Incorporación de interacción vocal en mundos virtuales usando VoiceXML*, CEIG, 2004
6. Bowman, D. A., Kluijff, E., Laviola, J., Poupyrev I., *3d User Interfaces. Theory and Practice*. Addison Wesley 2005
7. McGlashan, S., Axling, T., *Talking to Agents in Virtual Worlds*, UK VR-SIG Conf., 1996
8. VoiceXML Forum. "Voice eXtensible Markup Language": http://www.voicexml.org (Last access: June 2008)
9. Extensible 3D (X3D): http://www.web3d.org (Last access: June 2008)
10. Hartman, J., Wernecke, J., *The VRML 2.0 Handbook*, Silicon Graphics, 1994
11. SALT Technical White Paper: http://www.saltforum.org/whitepapers/whitepapers.asp (Last access: June 2008)
12. XHTML+Voice Profile 1.2: http://www.voicexml.org/specs/multimodal/x+v/12/spec.html (Revised at December 2007)
13. R. Dachselt. *BEHAVIOR3D: An XML-Based Framework for 3D Graphics Behavior*; ACM Web3D, 2003
14. VHML Standard: http://www.vhml.org (Last access: June 2008)
15. Latoschik, M.E. *Designing transition networks for multimodal VR-interactions using a markup language*, ICMI, 2002
16. Okazaki, N. et al. *An Extension of the Multimodal Presentation Markup Language (MPML) to a Three-Dimensional VRML Space*, Wiley-Interscience 2005
17. Carretero, M.P. et al. *Animación Facial y Corporal de Avatares 3D a partir de la edición e interpretación de lenguajes de marcas*, CEIG, 2004
18. XMMVR DTD: http://verbo.dcs.fi.uva.es/~holmedo/xmmvr/xmmvr.dtd
19. CORTONA: http://www.parallelgraphics.com/products/cortona/ (Last access: June 2008)
20. Phelps, A.M. *Introduction to the External Authoring Interface, EAI*. Rochester Institute of Technology, Department of Information Technology, http://andysgi.rit.edu/andyworld10/gallery/archives/vrml/media/eaiclass.doc (Revised at December 2006)
21. ATLAS IBERVOX: http://www.verbio.com (Last access: June 2008)
22. Multimodal Architecture and Interfaces: http://www.w3.org/TR/mmi-arch (Last access: June 2008)
23. COLLADA: http://www.collada.org (Last access: June 2008)
24. NICE: http://www.niceproject.com (Last access: June 2008)
25. CONTIGRA: http://www-mmt.inf.tu-dresden.de/Forschung/Projekte/CONTIGRA/index_en.xhtml (Revised at December 2007)
26. SAI, Scene Access Interface: http://www.xj3d.org/tutorials/general_sai.html (Last access: June 2008)
27. FreeWRL: http://freewrl.sourceforge.net (Last access: June 2008)
28. XJ3D: http://www.xj3d.org (Last access: June 2008)

Chapter 10
Designing User Interfaces for Collaborative Applications: A Model-Based Approach

María Luisa Rodríguez, José Luis Garrido, María Visitación Hurtado, Manuel Noguera, and Miguel J. Hornos

Abstract   For collaborative applications to be usable, their user interfaces should facilitate the process of sharing information within a group while carrying out common tasks. Currently, the design based on models is one of the most used techniques that seeks to assure high usability. In user interface design, models can describe and help to analyze abstract interface elements and relationships among them, as well as to guide the implementation using physical components. An approach for designing user interfaces using models at different abstraction levels is presented in this chapter. We also introduce a platform that provides a set of replicated components as a toolkit that facilitates the creation process of groupware user interfaces. In order to apply the proposal, we consider a case study based on a help system for risk operations in financial institutions. Specifically, the proposal aims at guiding the whole development process of user interfaces for collaborative applications.

10.1 Introduction

Traditionally, work is organized among groups in which some individuals interact with others in order to achieve a better productivity and performance. Users are part of a widely networked community and cooperate to perform their tasks. The discipline called CSCW (*Computer Supported Cooperative Work*) [1] studies and analyzes the coordination mechanisms of effective human communication and collaboration, as well as the systems supporting them. In the same vein, *groupware* is known as "computer-based system supporting groups of people engaged in a common task (or goal) and providing an interface to a shared environment" [4]. The development of collaborative applications, and therefore of multi-user interfaces, is more difficult than that of single-user applications given that social protocols and

M.L. Rodríguez (✉)
Dpto. de Lenguajes y Sistemas Informáticos, Universidad de Granada, E.T.S.I.I.T., C/ Periodista Daniel Saucedo Aranda, s/n, 18071 Granada, Spain
e-mail: mlra@ugr.es

J.A. Macías et al. (eds.), *New Trends on Human–Computer Interaction*,
DOI 10.1007/978-1-84882-352-5_10, © Springer-Verlag London Limited 2009

group activities involve to take into consideration additional elements for a successful design. As complex systems that they are, great efforts in modelling and development are required [1]. Hence, methodologies and implementation techniques which take into account group activities in addition to the interactions among people and computers must be applied.

The user interface of these systems must support the fulfillment of tasks in a collaborative manner within the group. This is not only an execution problem but also a design concern. In addition, the graphic user interface is a crucial aspect for the usability of collaborative applications, since it allows the improvement of communication, collaboration, and coordination among users interacting with the system. Therefore, new approaches should be applied for guiding the whole development process. Different methodologies and development environments based on models have been proposed in order to design user interfaces [16].

This research work aims to analyze and propose a model-based approach to the design of multi-user interfaces for collaborative applications. The focus of the chapter is on the definition and use of some relevant models, which provide support for the design of multi-user interfaces.

This chapter is organized as follows. Section 9.2 provides a review of some methodological approaches related to interactive and collaborative systems. Section 9.3 presents our approach to the design of multi-user interfaces for groupware applications. Section 9.4 outlines the main characteristics of a platform for the design of groupware interfaces. In Section 9.5 an application example of the approach described is shown. Finally, conclusions and future work are given in Section 9.6.

10.2 Background

User interface is "the part of the computer system allowing user to accede to computer facilities" [2]. Users' perception of an application depends on this component and on the fact that users accept the software application.

The model-based design is being extensively applied to system development. The aim is to define high-level models which allow designers to specify and analyze software systems from a semantic oriented level rather than to begin immediately with their implementation. All the information necessary to develop user interfaces is explicitly represented with declarative models.

Different user interfaces development proposals come from the interaction field, such as SUIP (Scenarios-based User Interface Prototyping) [5], IDEAS (Interface Development Environment within OASIS) [13], UMLi [18], TERESA (Transformation Environments for inteRactivE Systems representAtions) [15] and UsiXML [11]. Nevertheless, none of these previous proposals consider the development of collaborative systems, although other proposals address their development by means of the integration of some collaborative issues into the interactive system development. In [12], scenarios, requirements, and state machines are used to verify the interaction of some actors. In [3], a method to specify collaborative interactions among users is proposed. CIAM (Collaborative Interactive Applications Methodology) [14] allows user interfaces for groupware applications to be developed through the adoption of different points of view at the moment of approaching the creation of conceptual models for this kind of systems. TOUCHE [17] is a methodology for the development of user interfaces for groupware applications from the requirements gathering up to the implementation stage.

AMENITIES [6] is another methodology which allows to address systematically the analysis and design of CSCW systems and which facilitates subsequent software development. This methodology is based on behavior and task models, specially devised for the analysis, design, and development of these systems. It allows the realization of a conceptual system model focused on the group concept covering the most significant aspects of its behavior (dynamism, evolution, etc.) and structure (organization, laws, etc.). Information in this cooperative model (social roles, user's tasks, domain elements, person-computer and person-person dialogs, etc.) is relevant to the creation of the user interface. However, it does not include any mechanism to derive the user interface, although it is a crucial aspect [2]. Consequently, next section presents our approach to multi-user interface design using a particular set of models.

10.3 An Approach to the Design and Development of User Interfaces for Collaborative Applications

A new approach in order to address the design and development of user interfaces for collaborative applications is presented below, see general schema shown in Fig. 10.1. The starting point of the approach proposed in this chapter are the models present in the AMENITIES methodology. In this methodology, the description of a cooperative system is made up of two sets of models [6, 7]:

1. *Models used in techniques to elicitate requirements.* The process for the capture and description of requirements is mainly accomplished by means of the application of ethnography and use case techniques.
2. *Cooperative model.* It is a conceptual model that describes and represents the basic structure and behavior of the complete cooperative system. This model is built hierarchically on the basis of other models, each one focused on providing a different view of the system. A structured method is proposed in order to build the cooperative model: Organization specification stage, role definition stage, task definition, and specification of interaction protocols stages.

Previous models embrace the intrinsic characteristics for this kind of systems focussing on the integration of individual and collaborative aspects of the interaction. Group work should be almost as natural as the standalone one, although in practice the complexity of the collaborative work is clearly established by additional factors to be taken into account for a more efficient collaboration: group dynamics, social issues, diversification of the context, availability of group awareness mechanisms, distributed cognition, etc.

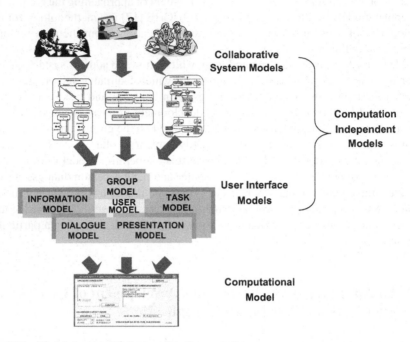

Fig. 10.1 Models involved in the user interfaces creation process

The second step explicitly establishes connections among collaborative models and the following specific models which are traditionally used for the development of user interfaces:

1. *Information model*: It defines the information domain of the application, i.e., the information objects managed by the application and the actions that they use.
2. *User model*: It describes the desired characteristics of the end user of the application to be developed, i.e., individual tasks associated to each role.
3. *Group model*: It describes the desired characteristics of the group of end users, i.e., the collaborative tasks and the context and environment for each group.
4. *Task model*: It defines all the tasks that end users perform in the application, i.e., types of tasks, roles associated to tasks, information objects required by tasks, temporal ordering of tasks, number of times in which each task is accomplished and number of actors involved in a task.
5. *Dialog model*: It describes the syntactic structure of human–computer interaction, i.e., actions on the interactive system and interaction protocols.
6. *Presentation model*: It determines the components that can appear on an end user's display and their layout characteristics, i.e., components to be included in the interface and their relationships.

Table 10.1 depicts connections among collaborative models and specific models useful in the creation of user interfaces.

Table 10.1   Connections among models

Amenities models	Models for user interface					
	Information	User	Group	Task	Dialog	Presentation
Applied ethnography	X	X	X	X	X	X
Use cases	–	X	–	X	–	X
Organization specification	–	X	X	X	–	X
Role definition	X	X	X	X	–	X
Task definition	X	X	X	X	X	X
Interaction Protocols	–	–	X	X	X	X

The objective of the next step, i.e., the design process, is to derive specific computation models of special interest in the building of multi-user interfaces. Relationships among the models described above (and shown in Table 10.1) identify the abstract interface elements to be taken into account. In turn, these elements and their relationships will be mapped onto elements of a computation model. For instance, the concepts and relationships of an organization diagram determines respectively:

- The role to be played by each member involved in the collaborative system. This information is relevant from the point of view of the group, user and presentation models (according to Table 10.1), which suggests to take some kind of design decision to fulfill this requirement. At the computational model level, it might be supported by providing a different interface for each role defined in the system.
- The change of the role that a user is granted to play in the system. The same previous models as well as the task model would be affected. The relationships specified in the organization diagram involve a mechanism to reflect the dynamic role change in the user interface, such as a graphical component for selecting the new role from a list of available roles. Subsequently, further design decisions lead to adapt the interface to the current setting, for example, adding a particular button associated to a new collaborative task. In other words, the user interface changes its static structure (components and characteristics, as enabled/disabled, visible/hidden, etc.) and behavior (navigation, information input and output, etc.), according to the requirements of the collaborative system.

The last step consists of the creation of the concrete interface stemming from standard and physical components for collaborative applications (telepointers, list of online users, shared text boxes, etc.), i.e., a platform of multi-user widgets. The platform used will be introduced in next section.

10.4 Platform for the Creation of Multi-user Interfaces

Multi-user interfaces should support the interaction among members of a same group who are working together in a collaborative task. Furthermore, the system must provide mechanisms to fulfill the group awareness requirements. Group awareness can be defined as "the understanding of the activities of others, which provides a context for your own activity" [4, 8]. This implies the management of contextual information about who is present in the system, which tasks the on-line users are carrying out, what specific artifacts are being used, and so forth. Ceedthrough, which is the propagation of the effects of actions executed by other users in the shared part of the interactive system [2], is also a relevant characteristic. These requirements stress the need of providing suitable support to the creation of interfaces for collaborative applications. Accordingly, a multi-user widget platform accessible through an API [10] that aims to facilitate the development of multi-user interfaces has been developed. The platform consists of a set of standard components (buttons, menus, text field, etc.) and specific components for collaborative applications (telepointers, list of online actors, chat, etc.). Moreover, as the components can be replicated, their implementation assures a global consistent state in case of simultaneous interaction of several users. Table 10.2 depicts the current set of available specific components in the platform. The platform also includes a module to manage metainformation dynamically. It allows reflecting changes related to the collaborative model itself during the application execution. A similar toolkit including standard and specific widgets is MAUI (Multi-user Awareness UI) [9].

Table 10.2 Specific components implemented in the platform

Name	Functionality
DIChat	Chat for online users
DIRoleChange	Show current role and enable to change to others
DICurrentRole	Show only active roles
DIOnlineUserList	List online users
DIUserListRolePlayed	Show online users and the role played for each one
DIUserListSameRole	Show online users playing the same role
Telepointer	Show another user's pointer movements

10.5 Case Study

We consider a case study based on a help system for the decision of risk operations by financial institutions. We describe a business process to grant a mortgage which a client has applied for in a branch office. This process entails the collaborative participation of people from the staff of three different organizations: a branch office, a valuation office, and a notary office. The construction of the cooperative model of this example follows the four stages method explained in Section 10.3:

organization specification, role definition, task definition, and specification of inter-action protocols.

The case of study has three organizations: branch, valuation office, and notary office. The organizations diagrams, defined in the organization specification stage, are shown in Fig. 10.2 (a). The Branch organization has three roles: Bank Manager, Head of Risk, and Teller. Following the organization diagram, some members may dynamically change the roles they play as a result of various circumstances. One example of these requirements is that the organization imposes laws such as [*Absent(bankManager)*], i.e., the actor playing the *headOfRisk* role can play the *bankManager* role if the bank manager is absent. This change implies that the actor playing the *headOfRisk* role when playing the *bankManager* role can realize the bank manager tasks. These requirements described in the cooperative model are translated into this example using the component *DIRoleChange* of Fig. 10.3(a). This component allows the actor to change his/her role selecting the new role. The component *DIRoleChange* allows the user to change his/her role by pressing the *Change* button. In a dialogue model, this is specified as an interaction between the user and the user interface. As a consequence, the user interface adapts to the new situation, showing the new *bankManager* role and the new *Give Approval* task. We use a formal method, MOORE (Model Oriented to Objects, Relationships and Manipulative Processes), to specify the user interaction, i.e., dialog model. It is based on a direct manipulation style in order to highlight relevant system features and properties [19].

```
Precondition:(Role = headOfRisk) ∧ (Absent(bankManager))
        ∃! m ∈ domain(mice), ∃! button_change ∈ domain(buttons):
        (m on button_change) ∧ click_m
Postcondition:(Role = bankManager) ∧ (show(button_giveapproval))
```

In general, this law in an organization diagram involves a mechanism to reflect the dynamical change role in the user interface. It is possible to carry out it by means of the *DIRoleChange* component, as in this case, or it can come by the execution of the system itself.

In task definition stage, each task previously specified is subdivided into related subactivities and actions required to achieve the objective. Figure 10.2(b) defines *mortgageGranting* task using COMO-UML task diagrams. The notation allows specifying temporal-ordered constraints of subactivities. Bifurcations denote a context-based decision in the organization. Each subactivity/action includes the specification of the responsible roles needed to accomplish it, for example the subactivity *decideConcession* is realized by the *bankManager* and *headOfRisk* roles. This is a collaborative task because more than one participant is required to accomplish it; therefore, all responsible roles must know who is using the system, where they are working and what they are doing at that moment. To implement this restriction of the cooperative model, the user interface of each participating role has to contain the necessary information about the work context of this task. This collaboration requirement will be satisfied with the replicated components shown in Fig. 10.3: *DIUserListRolePlayed* (b), *DIUserListSameRole* (c), and *DICurrentRole* (d).

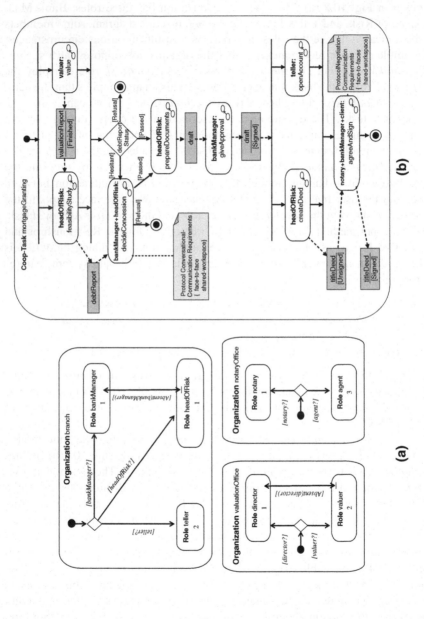

Fig. 10.2 Organization and task diagrams in COMO-UML

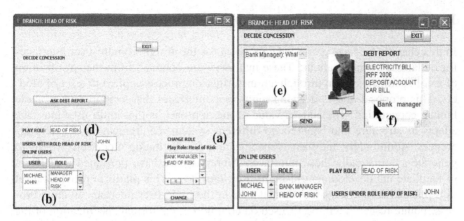

Fig. 10.3   User interfaces for subactivity *decideConcession*

In the last stage, the interaction protocols among participants must be identified and described. These protocols identify system requirements such as the type of (synchronous and asynchronous) communication required and the type of communication channel (link, mail, etc.) for supporting collaboration. In particular, the subactivity *decideConcession* specifies two communication requirements to accomplish it: a shared workspace exists, and each participant can see the others. In Fig. 9.3 we can observe the user interface of the subactivity *decideConcession*, which presents a shared workspace (the *Debt Report*) and a *DIChat* component (e) to implement the interaction between the actor playing the *bankManager* role and the actor playing the *headOfRisk* role. Moreover, we observe a *Telepointer* component (f) on debt report corresponding to the action of the actor playing the *bankManager* role at that moment. Table 10.3 shows the connections among the models for the case study.

Table 10.3   Mapping among the models for the case study

Cooperative Model	Models for user interface					Computational Model
	User	Group	Task	Dialog	Presentation	
Organization diagram						
Role change Task diagram	X	X	X	–	X	*DIRoleChange*
Collaborative task	–	X	X	X	X	*DIUserListRolePlayed* *DIUserListSameRole* *DICurrentRole*
Interaction protocols						
Type	–	–	X	X	X	*DIChat*
Shared-workspace	–	–	X	X	X	*DITelepointer*

10.6 Conclusions and Future Work

In this chapter, we have presented a proposal for the design of multi-user interfaces for collaborative applications. These interfaces are obtained from the specification of a collaborative system through a transformation process applied to a set of models. This proposal allows deriving multi-user interfaces that support and promote human cooperation. The add-on value of the approach is that multi-user interface adapts its structure and behavior to different system requirements and user preferences. Additionally, the formal specification for the dialog model enables us to generate automatically these interfaces. Moreover, we have presented a platform to facilitate the development of multi-user interfaces. This platform provides a set of replicated components that can be used in the multi-user interface creation process. Future research will be focused on completing the formal specification of the system and on building a CASE tool for supporting the system modeling and the subsequence semi-automatic generation of user interfaces. Furthermore, we plan to carry out a usability evaluation of the collaborative user-interfaces developed by using experimental and heuristic techniques.

Acknowledgments This research has been supported by R+D projects of the Spanish CICYT TIN2008-05995/TSI

References

1. Beaudouin-Lafon, M. (ed.): Computer Supported Cooperative Work. John Wiley&Sons, Paris (1999)
2. Dix, A., Finlay, J., Abowd, G., Beale, R.: Human–Computer Interaction. Prentice-Hall (1998)
3. Dumont, A., Pietrobon. C.: A Method for Specification of Collaborative Interfaces through the Use of Scenarios. In: Proceedings of Fifth International Conference on CSCW in Design, pp. 15–19 (2001)
4. Ellis, C.A., Gibbs, S.J., Rein, G.L.: Groupware: Some Issues and Experiences. Commun. ACM **34**(1), 38–58 (1991)
5. Elkoutbi, M., Khriss, I., Keller, R.K.: Generating User Interface Prototypes from Scenarios. In: Proceedings of the Fourth IEEE International Symposium on RE, pp. 1–25 (1999)
6. Garrido, J.L., Gea, M., Rodríguez, M.L.: Requirements engineering in cooperative systems. In: Requirements Engineering for Sociotechnical Systems, pp. 226–244. Idea Group, Inc., USA (2005)
7. Garrido, J.L., Noguera, M., González, M., Hurtado, M.V., Rodríguez, M.L.: Definition and use of Computational Independent Models in an MDA-based groupware development process. Sci. Comput. Program. **66**(1), 25–43 (2007)
8. Grudin, J.: Groupware and Cooperative Work: Problems and Prospects. In: Baecker, R.M. (ed.) Readings in Groupware and CSCW, pp. 97–105. Morgan Kaufman Publishers, San Mateo, CA (1993)
9. Hill, J.M.: A Direct Manipulation Toolkit for Awareness Support in Groupware. PhD Thesis, University of Saskatchewan (2003)
10. Ibáñez Santórum, J.A.: Diseño e implementación de una plataforma para el desarrollo de sistemas groupware. Proyecto fin de carrera. Dpto. Lenguajes y Sistemas Informáticos, University of Granada (2006)

11. Limbourg, Q., Vanderdonckt, J., Michotte, B., Bouillon, L., López-Jaquero, V.: UsiXML: A Language Supporting Multi-Path Development of User Interfaces. Lect. Notes Comput. Sci. **3425**, 200–220 (2005)
12. López Nores, M., et al.: Formal Specification Applied to Multiuser Distributed Services: Experiences in Collaborative t-Learning. J. Syst. Softw. **79**(8), 1141–1155 (2006)
13. Lozano, M.: Entorno Metodológico Orientado a Objetos para la Especificación y Desarrollo de Interfaces de Usuario. Tesis Doctoral, Universidad Politécnica de Valencia (2001)
14. Molina, A.I., Redondo, M.A., Ortega, M.: Conceptual and Methodological Framework for Modelling Interactive Groupware Applications. Lect. Notes Comput. Sci. **4154**, 413–420 (2006)
15. Mori, G., Paternò, F., Santoro, C.: Design and Development of Multidevice User Interface through Multiple Logical Description. IEEE Trans. Softw. Eng. **30**(8), 507–520 (2004)
16. Paternò, F.: Model-Based Design and Evaluation of Interactive Applications. Springer-Verlag, London (1999)
17. Penichet, V.: Task-Oriented and User-Centred Process Model for Developing Interfaces for Human-Computer-Human Environments. PhD. Thesis, Universidad de Castilla-La Mancha (2007)
18. Pinheiro da Silva, P., Paton, N.W.: UMLi: The Unified Modelling Language for Interactive Applications. Lect. Notes Comput. Sci. **1939**, 117–132 (2000)
19. Rodríguez, M.L., Rodríguez, M.J., Gea, M.: A Framework for Modelling the User Interface with a Complex System. Lect. Notes Comput. Sci. **2809**, 50–61 (2000)

Chapter 11
Evaluation of Text Input Techniques in Immersive Virtual Environments

Gabriel González, José P. Molina, Arturo S. García, Diego Martínez, and Pascual González

Abstract This chapter describes six different text input techniques and their evaluation. Two techniques stand out from the others. First, a mobile phone keyboard turn out to be a valuable option, offering high typing speed and low typing errors. Second, handwritten character recognition did not perform as good as expected. All findings from this and previous experiments are collected in a proposed guidance tool which will promote their application in future projects.

11.1 Introduction

Many advances in 3D User Interface (3DUI) design have been brought by proposing and evaluating different techniques to known tasks. Three universal tasks have been identified: navigation, selection, and manipulation. Some authors also add system control and symbolic input to them [1]. In Immersive Virtual Environments (IVEs), there are many situations where symbolic data input, such as text and numbers, is required, but the use of a Head-Mounted Display (HMD) and the upright position of the user—both characteristics of these systems—are incompatible with the use of a conventional keyboard. First, the use of a HMD prevents the user from seeing the surrounding real world, so the user must rely on the visual information displayed by the HMD, or on other senses such as touch to operate real world devices for that task. Second, the upright position requires light devices that can be carried or worn by the user.

To enable text input in such systems, different techniques have been proposed, from using small keyboards to speech recognition. In [1], proposals are classified into four categories: pen-, keyboard-, gesture-, and speech-based techniques.

J.P. Molina (✉)
Laboratory of User Interaction and Software Engineering (LoUISE), Instituto de Investigación en Informática de Albacete (I3A), Universidad de Castilla-La Mancha, Campus universitario s/n – S-02071 Albacete (Spain)
e-mail: jpmolina@dsi.uclm.es

J.A. Macías et al. (eds.), *New Trends on Human–Computer Interaction*,
DOI 10.1007/978-1-84882-352-5_11, © Springer-Verlag London Limited 2009

In this chapter, six different techniques are presented, highlighting the use of a mobile phone keyboard by its novelty in IVEs, and the handwritten character recognition by its complex implementation. The selection of the techniques has been done in order to evaluate as many different types of them as possible, and also taking into account performance factors such as speed and typing errors.

11.2 Description of the Evaluated Techniques

In order to perform an abstract and general task such as symbolic input in a particular system, a concrete implementation is required. That particular implementation is known as an Interaction Technique (ITe), defined as the way some input and/or output devices are used to carry out an interaction task. Then, this section will review each one of the ITes implemented and evaluated in our study.

11.2.1 Low-Key Count Keyboards

Many devices employed for the symbolic input tasks are indeed miniaturized or simplified versions of other devices used in conventional text input, mainly keyboards. Making the keyboard small enough by reducing the number of keys is the solution used in cell phones and other handheld devices, such as the Twiddler2.

11.2.1.1 Mobile Phone Keyboard

Today mobile phones feature a long list of functions that require text input, but these are based on a simple number-pad with 12 or 15 keys that can be held in one hand while tapping the keys with the thumb. Each key is assigned a set of symbols, and the user selects a symbol from each set by making multiple taps on the same key. When several symbols assigned to the same key need to be entered, the user must wait some time between each symbol.

Bearing in mind the widespread of mobile phones and this ITe with them, it is straightforward to think in translating its application to IVEs. A PC number-pad has the same number of keys and is not too large or heavy. A small programmable keyboard is preferred, such as the X-keys Desktop by P.I. Engineering, Inc. [2], suiting our needs with its 20 customizable keys, although only 9 of them will be used—those located at the bottom-right part of the keyboard, which are suitable for right-handed people—so that all of them can be reached by the user with their thumb while that hand is handling the keyboard. The symbol mapping matches the one of a cell phone, allowing the user to insert a blank space by pressing the '1'-key. As the HMD prevents the user from looking at any real object, and in order to help them to identify which key is under their thumb, embossed labels were stuck onto each key surface (left image in Fig. 11.1).

11.2.1.2 Chord Keyboards

These keyboards offer all the functionality of a full-size keyboard, but with fewer keys. With these keyboards, the user presses multiple keys at the same time to send one character. The set of keys pressed is called a "chord." In general, it takes time to operate it efficiently, because the location of symbols differs from a conventional QWERTY keyboard. In our case, the selected device for this technique is the Twiddler2 (Fig. 11.1, central image), by Handykey Corp. [3]. As an advantage, this chord keyboard can be operated in an upright position with only one hand.

Fig. 11.1 X-keys pad (*left*), twiddler2 (*center*) and pinch keyboard (*right*)

11.2.2 Pinch Keyboard

Described in [4]—also in [1] and [5]—this technique benefits from the users' experience with QWERTY keyboards, and is based on the Pinch Glove system, by Fakespace Systems Inc. [6]. This system comprises a couple of light gloves with conductive cloth on each fingertip which are used for detecting whether two of them are in contact, which is known as a "pinch" gesture. Thus, the technique relies on that gesture to interpret that a key has been pressed by the user. More precisely, with the left hand over the central row (the reference one), the contact between the little finger and the thumb is interpreted as pressing the 'a'-key on a standard QWERTY keyboard, between the index and the thumb as the 'f'-key and so on.

In order to detect over which row is located each hand, and also when the inner keys are pressed, the gloves need to be complemented with a pair of 6-DOF sensors—not included in the Pinch Glove system—so that the position and orientation of the hands are also tracked. Selecting a row on the keyboard is done by moving the hands toward the body (bottom row and space) or taking them away from it (top row). As for the inner columns (which include the 'G' and 'H'), keys are selected by rotating the hands inward, around the direction that the user is heading. Right image in Fig. 11.1 shows one user entering text with this ITe, wearing a HMD, and a pair of gloves. In the virtual environment, user's hands are represented with yellow cubes.

11.2.3 Pen and Tablet Technique

The last three techniques share the same hardware requirements, making it possible to implement them together in the same application. These ITes are based on a light tablet that the user holds in one hand, while the other handles a pen-shaped object. In our case, both elements are made of wood and have a piece of Velcro® to attach a position and orientation sensor. Sensors are used to match these physical objects with their corresponding virtual versions displayed in the HMD. If the calibration is good enough, the visual image provided by the HMD will be augmented through the sense of touch by the corresponding contact in the real world.

Fig. 11.2 Pen-based QWERTY and disk keyboard (*left*) and character recognition (*right*)

11.2.3.1 Pen-Based QWERTY Keyboard

With software-based keyboards the user presses virtual keys instead of physical ones in order to input different symbols, which allows an easy reconfiguration of the key layout or the symbol alphabet. Some PDA devices provide keyboards like this, displaying a QWERTY keyboard on the touch screen. With a pen and a tablet it is easy to translate this technique to IVEs (Fig. 11.2, top left image). However, text input is constrained to one symbol each time, and the user will not be able to feel the keys as she does with a conventional QWERTY keyboard.

11.2.3.2 Pen-Based Disk Keyboard

This ITe is much like the one described before, again a software-based keyboard over the surface of the tablet. However, this time the keys are placed around a disk as in the Cirrin system [7]. In the implemented technique, the user moves the pen to the desired symbol, drags the pen over the tablet surface to the disk center and then the symbol is sent (Fig. 11.2, bottom left image). After moving the pen over a symbol, the user can cancel the selection by moving the pen away from the disk.

This is important when a low rate of errors is desired, as the user must "confirm" the selection.

11.2.3.3 Handwritten Character Recognition

The last ITe relies on computer algorithms to recognize handwritten symbols, similarly to the Virtual Notepad system described in [8], but this time the characters are recognized individually and not as part of a word. Following previous developments, such as [9], this work is based on linear Hidden Markov Models (HMMs) with discrete outputs. In contrast to "off-line" recognition addressed in [9], in this work the input data is processed as is generated ("on-line" recognition).

Thus, each character is associated to a model, and the number of states defined for each model equals the minimum number of segments that are required to write that character. For instance, the character 't' can be written with two crossed strokes, and so its model is formed by four states. The recognition algorithm then computes the probability of generation of the observations for each model, determining which handwritten character has a higher probability of generating the observed features. This work follows a language-independent approach, that is, each symbol has a priori the same probability. To find the optimum number of states, Viterbi's algorithm was also implemented. As for the training procedure, it is based on Baum-Welch's algorithm to tune the parameters of each model to the sample characters. The pattern vectors calculated through training sessions are also used in the implemented recognition method, achieving a higher success ratio by summing the probability computed by the HMM and the similarity of input data to pattern vectors.

11.3 Description of the Experiment

The purpose of this experiment is to put into practice each implemented ITe with real users, gathering two types of data: quantitative and qualitative. A similar experiment is described in [4]. That time, four text input techniques were tested: the Pinch Keyboard, a pen and tablet keyboard, a chord keyboard, and speech recognition. For the latter, the authors used a "wizard of Oz" approach, that is, no actual speech recognition software was used. This time, the number of techniques is higher, and a different experiment design has been chosen for their evaluation.

11.3.1 Task Design

According to [10], there are three methods of planning an experiment: independent subject design, matched subject design, and repeated measures. The first method was used in [4], dividing 28 participants in four groups of 7, each one testing one single text input technique. However, doing it that way no participant can tell which ITe liked the most. Instead, the third method was preferred for our experiment, that is, the same group of participants would repeat the same task one time for each technique. As a trade-off, each user also took more time to complete the experiment, and special attention must be paid so that fatigue or learning did not affect the results in a negative way.

In order to test the implemented techniques, a text input task was prepared, which consisted of a set of sentences that participants had to enter. The sentences were chosen so that all the letters were represented. Their length and number were chosen so that writing the sentences took enough time to obtain significant results, but not too much to cause fatigue to participants.

The independent variables were the user, the ITe, and the sentence to write, that is, the conditions that characterizes each trial. The dependent quantitative variables are three: time to complete each sentence, number of characters typed per minute, and number of typing errors. As a dependent qualitative variable, subjective comfort was gathered through questionnaires.

11.3.2 Hardware and Software

A Kaiser ProView XL35 helmet, an Ascension Flock of Birds tracking system, and a Fakespace Pinch Gloves system were used in this experiment (Figs. 11.1 and 11.2, right image), all of them connected to a HP workstation with a NVIDIA Quadro4 900 XGL graphics card. The operating system was MS Windows XP, and the applications were developed in C++ language using MS Visual Studio 7.0 (.NET 2002), making use of the programming library VR Juggler 2.0 [11]. This library makes it easy to manage the VR devices, through the Gadgeteer component. For the representation of the objects in the virtual world, OpenGL primitives were used, together with some functions from GLUT. Finally, the computations related to the handwritten character recognition were supported by a library named as ARPREC [12], in order to push the precision beyond the limits of the type double in C++.

11.3.3 Subjects

The total number of participants that took part in our experiment was 10, being all of them students recruited from undergraduate courses. There were 7 males and 3 females, with ages ranging from 20 to 30 years old. All participants were technically literate, but had not previous experience in IVEs.

11.3.4 Experiment Procedure

All ITes were tested in the same virtual world, which represents a room. Within that room, a table is found, and there are some aids or guides placed to help users perform the trials. There is also a blackboard on a wall, where entered text is drawn. Other elements are the user's hands (if gloves are worn) and the pen and tablet (for the techniques that require them). As these last elements have also a correspondence in the real world, in particular with a table at our lab, special care is taken to match the dimensions, so that the visual perception of the virtual world is appropriately augmented with touch.

Each participant was given a description of the IVE and also instructions regarding the task to complete. For each ITe, participants were instructed about its usage, and then they were free to enter text for a period of time before the trials.

For each trial, each user had to enter a sentence as they listened to it. There were 10 different sentences, between 20 and 28 characters long, summing 239 characters in total. To minimize the learning effect, not only each participant followed a different order of ITes, but also the order of the sentences was different for each ITe. When a user failed to write the correct character, she did not correct it, but instead she went on with the trial typing the following character, so that mistakes have no influence on the characters typed per minute.

Questionnaires were used to gather the opinion of the participants, structured in three subsections: data about the user, age, genre, etc., data common to all techniques, devices, fatigue, etc., and data specific to each technique, i.e. the frequency of use of cell phone keyboards to enter text, particularly short messages. To answer the questions, the participant chose a value from a 1 to 5 scale.

11.3.5 Results of the Experiment

The first result to remark is that the ITe based on a mobile phone keyboard turn out to be the best as typing speed regards (Fig. 11.3, left chart), although this speed varies depending on the experience of the user with those devices, from 32.75 to 107.39 cpm for the 10 sentences. This relation is confirmed when comparing the number of characters per minute with the frequency of use of cell phone keyboards to enter text, given by users in the questionnaires with a value from 1 (never) to 5 (frequently). This results in a correlation factor of 0.85.

The next best techniques in typing speed are those two that represent a standard QWERTY keyboard: the one based on pen and tablet, and the Pinch Keyboard. From these two techniques, the worst one is the latter, even though it allows the user to quickly reach any letter in the keyboard, the users faced some problems when using this technique, possibly because they were not really used to type using all the fingers of both hands over a QWERTY keyboard.

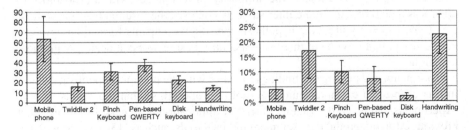

Fig. 11.3 Characters per minute (left) and typing errors (right) for each technique

As regards the number of typing errors (Fig. 11.3, right chart), the disk keyboard based on pen and tablet is the one that presents the lowest values. This is because it allows the user to think twice before sending a character, dragging the pen to the center button or moving it away from the disk. Another technique that stands out in this aspect is the phone keyboard, resulting in an average number of errors around 3 per cent. The fact that the user can tap the same key multiple times until the desired symbol appears again can be a reason for that good result.

On the opposite, the ITes that worst results obtained, both in number of typing errors and number of characters typed per minute, are the chord keyboard (Twiddler2) and the handwriting technique. In the case of the chord keyboard, it was not only qualified by users as the most difficult to learn, but also the users faced severe problems when positioning their fingertips over the correct combination of keys. Regarding handwriting, the number of typing errors is even higher than the previous technique, which can be explained if we take into account that users had some problems to write down each letter as similar as possible to the provided samples, and was made worse by the recognition errors due to the algorithm itself.

Finally, as for the qualitative data, the users considered the HMD as the most uncomfortable device, and identified the neck as the part of the body where most of them suffered from fatigue. This can be caused by the continued use of the helmet—it was employed in all the trials—or the need to move the head down to the tablet or the table, where aids and guiders where placed.

11.4 An Exemplar Guidance Tool

The experiment carried out expands the work described in [4] with three new text input techniques: mobile phone keyboard, pen and tablet disk keyboard, and handwritten character recognition. The general conclusion is the same in both studies, that is, none of the ITes is better than the others in every aspect. This finding can also be checked by performing a two-way ANOVA (ANAlisys Of VAriance), with the following parameters: $n = 10$ (number of users), $K = 6$ (number of techniques), and $N = 60$ (total number of samples, in this case average values computed for each trial and each user). As for the inter-groups analysis, the result is $F(5, 45) = 34.11$, $p < 0.05$, which rejects the similarity of techniques with a probability of error less than 0.05. As for the inter-subjects analysis, the result is $F(9, 45) = 1,51$, $p > 0.05$, which confirms the hypothesis that the participants formed an homogeneous group, that is, none of them was specially best or worst at dealing with these techniques.

To sum up, and putting our findings together with the previously published study, in this chapter an exemplar guidance tool is proposed, so that the results of both experiments can be easily used by other VR application designers, following other previous efforts in producing exemplar guidance tools, such as [13–15]. Particularly, this tool is a decision tree (Fig. 11.4).

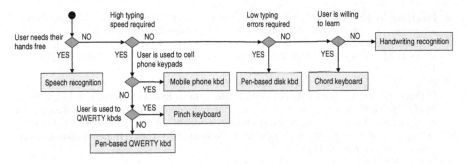

Fig. 11.4   VE design guidance tool for text input techniques

11.5 Conclusions and Further Work

In this chapter, the implementation and evaluation of six different ITes to carry out the task of symbolic input in IVEs has been described. In addition to that, results have been compiled in an exemplar guidance tool, which is the main contribution of this work. From the obtained results, there is one technique that stands out regarding the typing speed, which is the mobile phone keyboard, which benefits from the widespread of those devices in everyday life. Another technique that suspasses the others by its low number of typing errors is the disk keyboard based on pen and tablet. Besides, even though its results are not quite good, this study has also included a handwriting technique. Based on these conclusions, a tool has been proposed in the form of a decision tree that helps designers find the most appropriate technique. Further studies could include other ITes such as text prediction (e.g., T9 [16]), or make use of the implementation of HMM to recognize sign language. Then, future findings could be accommodated in the proposed tool.

Acknowledgments   This work has been partially supported by the project CICYT TIN2004-08000-C03-01 funded by the Ministerio de Educación y Ciencia of Spain, and the project PAI06-0093 funded by the Junta de Comunidades de Castilla-La Mancha.

References

1. Bowman, D.A., E. Kruijff, J. LaViola, and I. Poupyrev. 3d user interfaces: theory and practice. Addison-Wesley, 2004.
2. P.I. Engineering. X-keys® Desktop (20 keys). URL: http://www.piengineering.com/xkeys/xkdesk.php
3. Handykey Corporation. Twiddler2. URL: http://www.handykey.com/site/twiddler2.html
4. Bowman, D.A., C.J. Rhoton and M.S. Pinho Text Input Techniques for Immersive Virtual Environments: an Empirical Comparison. In Proceedings of the Human Factors and Ergonomics Society Annual Meeting, pp. 2154–2158, 2002.
5. Bowman, D.A., C.A. Wingrave, J.M. Campbell and V.Q. Ly. Novel Uses of Pinch Gloves for Virtual Environment Interaction Techniques. In Virtual Reality Vol. 6, No. 2, pp. 122–129, 2002.

6. Fakespace Systems Inc. – Mechdyne Corporation. Pinch® Glove system. URL: http://www.
   mechdyne.com/integratedSolutions/displaySystems/products/Pinch/pinch.htm
7. Mankoff J., and G. Abowd. Cirrin: A Word-Level Unistroke Keyboard for Pen Input. In Proc.
   of the ACM Symposium on User Interface Software and Technology (UIST'98), pp. 213–214,
   1998.
8. Poupyrev, I., N. Tomokazu and S. Weghorst. Virtual Notepad: handwriting in immersive VR.
   In Proceedings of the Virtual Reality Annual International Symposium, pp. 126–132, 1998.
9. Bunke, H., M. Roth and E. Schukat-Talamazzini. Off-line Cursive Handwriting Recognition
   using Hidden Markov Models. In Pattern Recognition, Vol. 28, No. 9, pp. 1399–1413, 1995.
10. Preece, J., Y. Rogers, H. Sharp, D. Benyon, S. Holland and T. Carey. Human-Computer Inter-
    action. Addison-Wesley, 1994.
11. Juggler, V.R. URL: http://www.vrjuggler.org/
12. Bailey D.H., et al. ARPREC, C++/Fortran-90 arbitrary precision package. URL: http://crd.
    lbl.gov/˜dhbailey/mpdist/
13. Eastgate, R. The Structured Development of Virtual Environments: Enhancing Functionality
    and Interactivity. PhD Thesis. University of York, 2001.
14. García, A.S., J.P. Molina y P. González. Aproximación a la evaluación de interfaces de Reali-
    dad Virtual. Proc. of IV Congreso de Interacción Persona-Ordenador, Interacción '05, as part
    of CEDI'05, Granada, Spain, 2005..
15. Marsh, T., P. Wright, S. Smith and D. Duke. A Shared Framework of Virtual Reality. Proceed-
    ings of 5th UKVRSIG, Exeter, UK. 1998.
16. Tegic Communications Inc. T9 Text Input. URL: http://www.t9.com/

Chapter 12
Dealing with Abstract Interaction Modeling in an MDE Development Process: A Pattern-Based Approach

Francisco Valverde, Ignacio Panach, Nathalie Aquino, and Oscar Pastor

Abstract   Currently, in the Model-Driven Engineering (MDE) community, there is not any standard model to define the interaction between the user and the software system. However, the Human–Computer Interaction (HCI) community has been recently dealing with this issue. A widely accepted proposal is the specification of the interaction at two levels or views: an Abstract Level, in which the User Interface (UI) is defined without taking into account any technological details, and a Concrete Level, in which the previous abstract models are extended with the information related to the target technology. The purpose of this chapter is to introduce the Abstract Level into the OO-Method MDE development process. Specifically, this chapter is focused on how the abstract interaction can be modeled by means of Abstract Interaction Patterns (AIPs). These patterns define a generic solution for an interaction between a user and an Information System (IS), without considering the technological details related to the final UI. In order to illustrate the approach, two AIPs are described.

12.1 Introduction

Model-Driven Engineering is considered to be a promising approach for the development of Information Systems [13]. Following this paradigm, the software application can be automatically generated by means of a Conceptual Model. From this model, several transformations are applied to obtain the final system implementation. Since this approach improves software development, several model-based methods have been proposed from both academic and industrial environments. However, these methods have been mainly designed to model the functionality and persistency of the IS (business and data-base logic, respectively) pushing into the

F. Valverde (✉)
Centro de Investigación en Métodos de Producción de Software, Universidad Politécnica de Valencia, Camino de Vera S/N, 46022 Valencia, Spain
e-mail: fvalverde@pros.upv.es

J.A. Macías et al. (eds.), *New Trends on Human–Computer Interaction*,
DOI 10.1007/978-1-84882-352-5_12, © Springer-Verlag London Limited 2009

background the UI modeling. Nowadays, the UI is gaining enormous importance because the end-user can interact with software systems from a wide array of technological platforms (i.e., Desktop, Web, mobile devices, etc.) which have different interaction mechanisms. Therefore, the interaction modeling must be considered a key requirement in a MDE development process.

The HCI community has been dealing with UI modeling for a long time. Previous HCI approaches have defined mechanisms to specify interaction such as ConcurTaskTrees [12] or UI description languages [18]. A widely accepted proposal is to define the UI specification at two main levels: an Abstract Level, in which the UI is modeled without taking into account platform or technological details and a Concrete Level, where the previous abstract models are extended with the information related to the target platform. However, in general terms, the HCI community has not taken into account how the interaction specification must be linked with the underlying system functionality. Therefore, with the proposals of the HCI community, a prototypical UI can be automatically generated, while a fully functional application cannot.

The main purpose of this work is to define a bridge between both HCI and MDE principles in order to improve how the interaction is defined at the Conceptual Level. Combining the best practices from both communities, a model-driven approach that defines both the interaction and the underlying IS logic can be obtained. In this chapter, an Abstract Interaction Model is introduced as the first step to achieving this goal. The basic elements proposed to define this model are the Abstract Interaction Patterns, which describe an interaction between the user and the IS at the Conceptual Level. The use of patterns provides the analyst with a common modeling framework to define generic interaction requirements. Furthermore, the knowledge represented by AIPs is general enough to be applied in different model-based software development methods. As an example of application, the OO-Method software production method [11] has been chosen to illustrate how to include the Abstract Interaction Model on a MDE method. The main goal of this new Abstract Interaction Model is to improve the expressivity of the current OO-Method Presentation Model.

The rest of the chapter is structured as follows. Section 12.2 introduces the Abstract Interaction Model and describes two Abstract Interaction Patterns. Next, an overview of the OO-Method development process using the new Abstract Interaction Model is introduced. Section 12.4 compares the approach presented here with the related work. Finally, the concluding remarks are stated in Section 12.5.

12.2 Defining the Abstract Interaction Model: Abstract Interaction Patterns

In the context of this work, the interaction is defined as the communication flows between the user and the IS by means of a software interface. The main goal of the Abstract Interaction Model is to describe the interaction without considering technological concepts of the UI. In order to achieve this goal, the interaction is represented by users and tasks. On the one hand, users represent a set of human subjects (i.e., Anonymous user, Customer, etc.) who share the same interactions with the IS. On the other hand, a task (i.e., 'Payment introduction', 'Log to the system', etc.) specifies an interaction with the IS to reach a goal in a specific software application. In addition, each user is related to a set of tasks that define its available interactions.

In order to describe the interaction represented by each task, this work introduces the concept of Abstract Interaction Pattern. An AIP defines a generic solution for a common interaction scenario between the user and the IS using a Conceptual Model. Instead of defining the interaction in terms of the final UI components involved, these patterns model the reason why the user interacts with the IS. Two common examples of interaction are the retrieval of data (i.e., show the user the cars that are available for rent) or the execution of a service (i.e., the payment of the car rental). To define these two interactions, the AIP models must be associated with the underlying models of the IS that represent the data and functionality. Hence, interactions are modeled over the data and functionality that the IS provides to the users.

To precisely define an interaction, the UI elements or widgets (i.e., buttons, forms, input boxes, etc.) that are used to interact must be specified. However, these widgets should not be included in the Abstract Interaction Model because they are technologically dependent on the target platform. To avoid this issue, a subset of the Canonical Abstract Components [3] is used at the Abstract Level to identify the interface components involved in the interaction defined by an AIP.

The advantages of using a structured and organized pattern language have been previously stated [19]. Therefore, according to previous works on pattern language definition [6, 8], the AIPs have been defined using a pattern template with the following common sections: (1) A description of the *Problem* that the pattern is intended to solve; (2) The *Context* in which it is recommended to use the pattern; (3) A brief textual description of the proposed *Solution*, and (4) A real *Example* to show how the pattern can be applied. However, to apply these patterns in a model-driven development process, a more precise description is required. In particular, two main requirements must be satisfied:

1. The pattern should describe the entities and the properties of a Conceptual Model that abstracts the interaction. In the modeling step, that metamodel is instantiated as a model by the analyst to specify the required interaction in an application domain. In addition, the conceptual elements of that model are the source elements from which the model-to-code transformations are defined.
2. The pattern should include a precise description about the interaction expected in the final UI. This description must be used as a guideline to implement the model-to-code transformation rules, which generate the expected UI code when the pattern is applied.

With the aim of addressing both requirements, two more sections are introduced to the pattern template:

1. *Metamodel*: This defines the concepts that the pattern abstracts by means of a metamodeling language. Additionally, this metamodel must include a clear description of the different entities, relationships, properties, and constraints. The metamodel entities must also be related to the entities of the IS metamodel in order to establish the integration between interaction and functionality at the Conceptual Level. Therefore, the metamodel defines the static information used to create specific models of the pattern.

2. *Interaction semantics*: This precisely specifies the interaction expected when the pattern is applied. This section shows the analyst how the different conceptual elements of the metamodel must be translated to implement the interaction defined. Therefore, it describes the Abstract Interface Components [3], the interface events and the business logic objects involved in the interaction. Additional interaction models, such as UML Interaction Diagrams, CTTs or Scenarios, are recommended to provide a better understanding of the semantics represented. To sum up, this section describes the interaction behavior abstracted by the pattern.

One advantage of our proposal is that the concepts represented with AIPs are not coupled with a specific development method. As a consequence, these patterns can be used as guidelines to improve the interaction modeling in different model-based methods. Furthermore, new patterns detected in other approaches can be described as AIPs to promote reuse. To illustrate how this approach is applied, two AIPs are presented: the Service AIP and the Population List AIP. For reasons of brevity, a brief pattern summary is provided for sections one through four of the pattern template. In these examples, the *Essential MOF* [4] language has been used to build the pattern Metamodel, whereas CTTs have been used to define the Interaction Semantics as the JUST-UI approach proposes [9].

12.2.1 Service AIP

Pattern summary: This pattern abstracts the dialog between the user and the IS for the execution of an operation. That dialog can be subdivided into two basic interactions: the input of the operation argument values and the invocation of the operation. The interaction represented by this pattern can be applied in several tasks. For example, in an online rental service, the task "Create a new rental" can be defined using this pattern. The pattern application provides a form where the user can enter the different argument values of the 'Rent' operation (the car name, the delivery and return date, etc.). When the user accepts the data entered (i.e., by clicking a button) the new rental is created in the IS.

Metamodel: A *Service AIP* (See Fig. 12.1) is directly related to an operation and a set of *Input Arguments*. On the one hand, the *Input Argument* entity represents the input interface component in which the user must input the value for an operation argument. On the other hand, the operation represents a IS functionality that is composed of a set of *Arguments*. The value of these arguments is provided by the *Input Arguments* related to the *Service AIP*. Therefore, the *Service AIP* can be described as a view over a unique functionality provided by the IS. Finally, the *Launch Action* property of the *Service AIP* defines which interface component launches the operation execution.

Interaction Semantics: The first step of the interaction is the *Input of the Service Arguments* (see Fig. 12.2). This task is decomposed into several 'Input Arg' interactive tasks, according to the different *Input Arguments* defined in the model. The values can be inserted in any order as the operator (|||) means. When the required values have been introduced, the user should trigger an event interface (i.e., by clicking a button) to invoke the operation execution (*Launch Event* task). Finally, the *Execute Service* interactive task performs the operation with the values introduced in the previous tasks.

12.2.2 Population List AIP

Pattern summary: Frequently, to avoid the incorrect input of a value, the interface provides a list of values from which the user must make a selection. The Population AIP represents the following type of interaction: the selection and input of a value that has been previously retrieved from the IS. Taking into account the previous example, the 'Create a new rental' task, this pattern can be applied to the car named *Input Argument*. Hence, the interface provides all the cars available and the user only has to choose the desired value instead of typing it.

Metamodel: The Population List AIP can be associated to any metamodel entity that represents an input interaction. For instance, in Fig. 12.1 a relationship with

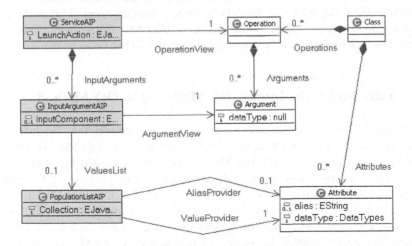

Fig. 12.1 Metamodels for the Service AIP and the Population List AIP

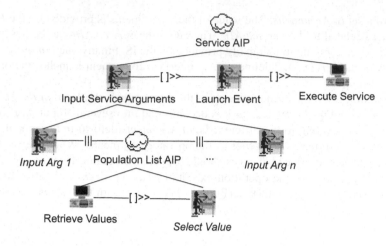

Fig. 12.2 ConcurTaskTree for the Service AIP and the Population List AIPs

an *Input Argument* has been defined. The pattern provides the property *Collection* to represent the interface component that shows the user the collection of values. These values are provided by a class *Attribute* that is associated with the pattern by means of the relationship *Value Provider*. The relationship *Alias Provider* can be optionally defined to show an alternative representation of the value to be selected. For example, if the value to be selected is the car numeric id, an alias that shows the car description instead of the id will be more intuitive for the end-user.

Interaction Semantics: First, the application task '*Retrieve Values*' (Fig. 12.2.) performs a query to the IS to retrieve the values of the *Value Provider* attribute defined in the *Class Attribute*. By default, these values are used to fill in the *Collection* property of the pattern, if there is not an *Alias Provider* defined. Finally, the interactive task '*Select Value*' represents the selection of the value by the user.

12.3 Introducing the Interaction Modeling in OO-Method

OO-Method [11] is an automatic code generation method that produces the equivalent software product from a conceptual specification. OO-Method provides a UML-based Platform-Independent Model, where the static and dynamic aspects of a system are captured by means of three complementary models: (1) The Object Model, which is defined as a UML Class Diagram; (2) The Dynamic Model, which is described as a UML Statechart Diagram, and (3) The Functional Model, which is specified using dynamic logic rules. Moreover, two approaches have been traditionally proposed to support the presentation modeling in OO-Method: the JUST-UI approach [8] which has been industrially implemented in the OLINAVOVA tool (www.care-t.com), and the OOWS Web Engineering Method [16] which provides Navigational and Presentational Models that are focused on the Web Application development domain. Concepts presented in both works have been taken into account to define the basis of the Abstract Interaction Model presented in this chapter. Therefore, the OO-Method Interaction Model is intended to be a unifying and extended proposal of the current Presentation Models.

The proposed OO-Method Interaction Model (see Fig 3.) describes the interaction using Conceptual Models (at the Problem Space) in order to automatically generate a Presentation Layer that represents the same interaction in programming code (at the Solution Space). Following the HCI principles, this Interaction Model is made up of two complementary views:

1. An Abstract View, which describes the different tasks that the user can perform with the IS in terms of AIPs introduced in the previous section. The AIP model entities are related to the OO-Method Object Model (the relationship *uses* in Fig. 12.3), which defines an interface with the data and the functionality from the IS. Hence, both models are integrated at the Conceptual Level.
2. A Concrete View defined as a set of Concrete Platform Interaction Patterns. These patterns are related to an AIP by means of a specialization relationship. Thus, their purpose is to extend the semantics of an abstract interaction with interaction concepts related to the target technological platform. In order to address concrete interaction requirements for different platforms, several Concrete Views can be defined (one per platform). The description of these patterns is beyond the scope of this chapter.

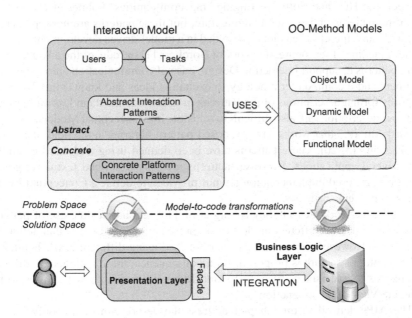

Fig. 12.3 Interaction model in the OO-method development process

Both views of the OO-Method Interaction Model are inputs of a model compiler which, according to a set of model-to-code transformation rules, produces the final Presentation Layer (See Fig. 12.3). Additionally, the generation of the Business Logic Layer for several technological platforms has been industrially implemented in the context of the OO-Method development process. Therefore, a fully functional application, not just the UI, can be generated with the integration of the two code generation processes.

12.4 Related Work

In the HCI community, some proposals, such as USIXML [18] and TERESA [10], have been made to model the interaction in an abstract way. In these works, the UI is designed independently of technological platform characteristics by means of ConcurTaskTrees [12]. Taking into account the principles proposed by the Chamaleon Framework [2], the UI is specified at different levels of abstraction. However, it is important to mention that both USIXML and TERESA can only represent the UI. Their abstract UI languages do not have the required expressiveness to generate the system functionality as OO-Method does. A recent approach for modeling the UI from the interaction perspective is the CIAM methodology [7]. However this methodology is mainly focused on the definition of Groupware UIs.

In the literature, there are other proposals based on patterns to represent the interaction. In the work presented by Folmer et al. [5], patterns are described as a bridge between the HCI and Software Engineering communities. Folmer et al. propose including patterns in the system architecture, but these patterns are not represented abstractly and, therefore, cannot be included in a model-driven development process. In the same line of reasoning, the work of Borchers [1] introduces the advantages of using patterns to support Interaction Design: ease of communication among all team members and a common terminology to exchange ideas and knowledge. Borchers proposes formal descriptions of the patterns in order to make them less ambiguous, but those descriptions are also difficult to translate into Conceptual Models.

Furthermore, other works have proposed pattern libraries in the field of Interaction Design [15, 20]. These patterns have been defined using real word examples from several applications. However, patterns are only described textually; guidelines or a proposed implementation are not provided to define a Conceptual Model to represent them abstractly.

Finally, the work presented by Sinnig et al. [14] emphasizes the use of patterns as building blocks of different models (task, presentation, and dialog) that define the interaction. However, these patterns are described using different XML languages and no pattern structure is proposed. As a consequence, these patterns are difficult for analysts to understand. Also, this work does not describe, how to represent the Concrete View of the interaction.

The AIPs defined in this chapter address the description of not only how to represent the interaction abstractly but also how the pattern can be applied in a

Model-Driven Environment. This approach extends the ideas proposed by Molina [9] and provides a more precise description of the pattern metamodel and the interaction semantics involved. In addition, our approach can be associated with a Concrete View that improves the expressivity of the patterns taking into account the target platform characteristics.

12.5 Concluding Remarks

In this chapter, an approach for improving interaction modeling has been presented. As several works state [9, 14], patterns are a recommended choice to represent the interaction in a model-driven development process. The presented AIPs provide a mechanism to promote the reuse of knowledge between different model-driven approaches and to guide the definition of the model-to-code generation process. The metamodel and the semantics that describe the interaction of the pattern are useful for integrating an AIP in different model-driven approaches. As a proof of concept, an Abstract Interaction Model that is related to the OO-Method approach has been defined.

A weakness of the approach is that there is no agreement on what the best model is to define the interaction semantics. Although in this chapter CTTs have been used, UML-based models may be more suitable to describe other AIP interaction semantics. Moreover, the introduction of the Concrete View may reveal the need for new conceptual primitives in the Abstract view.

It is important to mention two constraints of the proposal. First, this approach does not describe the aesthetic properties such as layout, fonts, colors, etc. Although it is true that characteristics of this type can have a great impact on the usability of the interaction, they should be addressed by another model. And secondly, the only modality of the interaction that is supported is carried out with common input/output devices.

Finally, further works will address the tool support required to define the Abstract Interaction Model in the OO-Method development process. As a previous step to reaching that goal, a metamodel of all the patterns must be developed together with the implementation of the corresponding model-to-code transformation rules. Furthermore, current work addresses how to define a Concrete view of the Interaction Model for modeling Rich Internet Applications.

Acknowledgments   This work has been developed with the support of MEC under the project SESAMO TIN2007-62894.

References

1. Borchers JO (2000) A Pattern Approach to Interaction Design. ACM Conference on Designing Interactive Systems – DIS, New York, United States:369–378
2. Calvary G, Coutaz J, Thevenin D, et al. (2003) A Unifying Reference Framework for multi-target user interfaces. Interacting with Computers 15(3):289–308

3. Constantine L (2003) Canonical Abstract Prototypes for Abstract Visual and Interaction Design. 10th International Workshop on Design, Specification and Verification of Interactive Systems (DSV-IS), Madeira, Portugal:1–15
4. EMOF Meta Object Facility 2.0 Core Proposal (2007). http//www.omg.org/docs/ad/03-04-07.pdf. Accessed 29 July 2008
5. Folmer E, van Welie M, Bosch J (2005) Bridging patterns: An approach to bridge gaps between SE and HCI. Information and Software Technology 48(2):69–89
6. Gamma E, Helm R, Johnson R, Vlissides J (1995) Design Patterns: Elements of Reusable Object-Oriented Software. Addison Wesley, Boston
7. Giraldo WJ, Molina AI, Collazos CA, Ortega M, Redondo MA (2008) CIAT, A Model-Based Tool for designing Groupware User Interfaces using CIAM. Computer-Aided Design of User Interfaces VI, Albacete, Spain:201–213
8. Molina PJ, Melia S, Pastor O (2002) JUST-UI: A User Interface Specification Model. Proceedings of Computer Aided Design of User Interfaces, Valenciennes, France:63–74
9. Molina PJ (2003). Especificación de interfaz de usuario: de los requisitos a la generación automática. Valencia, PhD Thesis. Universidad Politécnica de Valencia.
10. Mori G, Paterno F, Santoro C (2004) Design and Development of Multidevice User Interfaces through Multiple Logical Descriptions. IEEE Transactions on Software Engineering 30(8):507–520.
11. Pastor O, Molina JC (2007) Model-Driven Architecture in Practice: A Software Production Environment Based on Conceptual Modelling. Springer, Germany.
12. Paternò, F (2004) ConcurTaskTrees: An Engineered Notation for Task Models. The Handbook of Task Analysis for Human-Computer Interaction. Lawrence Erlbaum Associates, United Kingdom:483–501.
13. Schmidt DC (2006) Model-driven Engineering. IEEE Computer 39:26–31.
14. Sinning D, Gaffar A, Reichart D, Forbrig P, Seffah A (2005) Patterns in Model-Based Engineering. In: Computer-Aided Design of User Interfaces IV. S Netherlands: 197–210.
15. Tidwell J (2005) Designing Interfaces. O'Reilly Media, United States
16. Valverde F, Valderas P, Fons J, Pastor O (2007) A MDA-Based Environment for Web Applications Development: From Conceptual Models to Code. 6th International Workshop on Web-Oriented Software Technologies, Como,Italy:164–178
17. Valverde F, Panach JI, Pastor Ó (2007) An Abstract Interaction Model for a MDA Software Production Method. Tutorials, posters, panels and industrial contributions at the 26th international conference on Conceptual modeling Auckland, New Zealand 83:109–114
18. Vanderdonckt J, Limbourg Q, Michotte B, Bouillon L, Trevisan D, Florins M (2004) USIXML: a User Interface Description Language for Specifying Multimodal User Interfaces. Proceedings of W3C Workshop on Multimodal Interaction, Sophia Antipolis, Greece:1–12
19. van Welie M, van der Veer GC (2003) Pattern Languages in Interaction Design: Structure and Organization. Ninth IFIP TC13 International Conference on Human-Computer Interaction. Zurich, Switzerland:527–534
20. van Welie M (2007) Patterns in Interaction Design. http://welie.com. Accessed 29 July 2008 Accessed 29 July 2008

Chapter 13
WebA Mobile (Web Analysis Mobile): Assistance Tool for the Design and Evaluation of Websites for Mobile Devices

Luis Mena Tobar, Pedro Latorre Andrés, and Elena Lafuente Lapena

Abstract This chapter presents Mobile WebA (Assistance tool for the design and evaluation of sites for mobile devices), a new module of the WebA application developed by the Aragonese Usability Laboratory. This module facilitates the evaluation of usability and accessibility through the completion of the guidelines that are recommended by the best practices in the "W3C Mobile Web 1.0 Initiative," in addition to allowing the completion and analysis of relevant tests of user satisfaction.

13.1 Introduction

This chapter introduces Mobile WebA, a tool that responds to the changing needs of user interface designers that take into account the steady increase in the use of mobile devices.

Before presenting Mobile WebA, we want to discuss what motivated the development of this tool. Then, the theoretical issues that must be taken into account in evaluating the usability and accessibility of user interfaces for mobile devices are cited. The following sections are devoted to the existing systems to evaluate usability and accessibility and to "Best Practices in Mobile Web 1.0" [5], new patterns of the W3C [18], which represent a breakthrough for evaluating the accessibility of websites for mobile devices. Then WebA Mobile is explained. Finally, the findings and future development is presented.

In recent years, the offering of mobile devices that carry out operations which are normally made from a computer or laptop is growing considerably. Users want to access information from anywhere and from any device, despite the fact that mobile devices are still limited in resources. This causes that user experience is not entirely satisfactory, due to many problems encountered by accessing websites via mobile devices.

L.M. Tobar (✉)
Laboratorio Aragones de Usabilidad, Parque Tecnológico Walqa Ed.1. Cuarte (Huesca)
e-mail: luis@menasl.com

J.A. Macías et al. (eds.), *New Trends on Human–Computer Interaction*,
DOI 10.1007/978-1-84882-352-5_13, © Springer-Verlag London Limited 2009

The Aragonese Laboratory of Usability detected these problems and seeks to develop a tool to help developers create accessible and usable websites by all and on any device. This is how the idea of developing Mobile Web as a module of the WebA application came to be, and it is described in the following.

The goal of Mobile WebA is to help in the analysis and design of websites, verifying that access from any mobile device is as simple and convenient as it is from desktops or laptops. It takes into account the Mobile Web initiative, which seeks to solve the problems of interoperability and usability that currently impede access to the Web from mobile devices, and enable one of the main objectives that the W3C which consists of achieving an only Web (avoiding the need of different versions).

13.2 The Aragonese Usability Laboratory

The Aragonese Usability Lab [2] is an initiative of the General Directorate of Technologies for the Information Society of the Government of Aragon. Its activities are conducted on the premises of the Advanced Laboratory on Legal and Business implementation in Information Society [3] (Walqa Technological Park[10], Huesca), which is dependent on the Faculties of Law, Economics and Business Administration and the Superior Polytechnic Center of the University of Zaragoza.

The Laboratory develops R & D projects in the field of evaluating usability and accessibility of user interfaces, the results of which are applied in the study of consumer response to different stimuli, to improvement of usability in the design, and the evaluation of websites.

Among the R & D projects developed in the laboratory the highlight is WebA [19], a tool being used at present time to assess in a semi-automated way the accessibility and usability of websites, at the request of both public institutions and private companies.

13.3 Usability for Mobile Devices

The limitations of mobile devices from which users can access the Web are notable. The pocket PC or mobile phones have got smaller screen, less memory, and less processing speed than conventional computers.

If it is wished that the information for mobile users be useful, then the interface of websites must be defined more carefully and scrutinized in the devices from which users will be accessing the information. For example, a person must be able to access the most important sections from any page, and the very first page should show useful information for the user.

13.4 Usability vs. Mobile Characteristics

Due to limited memory and display of these devices, websites have to [15], among other things, show the most important and essential information (small screen and expensive connection) and minimize the length of the text to a maximum of three screen lengths (it is more difficult to scroll with the keyboard of a mobile phone). Also the use of tables is not desired (there are devices that cannot support them and depending how they have been created, they could be rendered outside the suitable width of the page), and only cache pages are rarely updated. Optimizing the dimension and size of graphics, and including alternative text function in all images are also important.

Another aspect which must be taken into account is the context of use of mobile devices. Users are in a dynamic environment, performing various tasks that can distract from the task at hand regarding the site. For example, while the user tries to buy tickets for a movie, make a bank transfer, etc. This is why the navigation structure has to be simple and avoid unnecessary steps.

Also, the task undertaken by the user on the website can be interrupted by other events. Depending on your mobile device a user could suffer loss of coverage, an incoming call, a distraction, etc. Therefore, the design should allow the process to be recovered after the interruption (return to the last page visited, with all the information that the user could have introduced, like a form).

In addition, it is necessary to take into account several economic issues: users know that they pay for time and/or traffic and they believe that it is expensive. Moreover, they are not convinced that it is secure and they connect to perform specific tasks, so the information should be brief and important.

Mobile devices have some physical characteristics that adversely affect the usability of a website, such as difficulty to write text, the size of the keys, the screen, the bandwidth, and instability of the connection. However, the most serious problem is the heterogeneity of devices (especially in mobile phones)

13.5 Usable Design in Mobile Devices

During the design process of a website for a mobile device, several criteria should be taken into account [15]. For example, writing on mobile devices is difficult and it is preferable to have selection of options than writing, even if there are extra steps. Also, only show relevant information and avoid the use of blank lines because it can cause the user to think that there is nothing below the line and the structure of the site should be simple.

It is not convenient to use multimedia content and flashy visual effects because embedded objects or script are not supported always and in many cases it is not possible to load plug-ins to add support. This applies in particular to advertising space.

It is advisable to reduce the number of keystroke in the implementation of each task. This affects the introduction of text, vertical scrolling, menu deployment, the default keys offered by the mobile device (softkeys), etc. It is not advisable to disable the native "back" function, which may go back to the previous page possible, but it is advisable to add a link to the "back" browser on all screens. Thus, users will be able to easily find the "back" feature.

In these devices, the limitations of the browser and the usability become critical. Some mobile devices are perceived as slow and expensive, their screens are small, and the different existing mechanisms (softkeys, navikeys, etc.) make navigation extremely difficult for data entry. These limitations, together with the variety of devices and browsers, imply that the design of a generic version is almost unattainable.

13.6 Web Accessibility for Mobile Devices

Accessibility is the set of characteristics which should be provided in an environment, product or service to be usable in terms of comfort, security and equality for all people and in particular for those with disabilities [13] (Accessibility National Plan 2004–2012).

Human beings are different from one another and all user interfaces should accommodate these differences so that anyone would be able to use it without problems. It is necessary to avoid design features only in response to specific population groups, imposing unnecessary barriers that could be avoided by paying sufficient attention to these issues.

Web accessibility means that anyone can access the website, regardless of hardware, software, language, and/or capabilities that the user may have. It is not difficult to enter a website from a mobile device, but economic and technical issues limit that access.

Access to a website from a mobile device can be done from anywhere, but these devices have a number of disadvantages. First of all, keyboard with few functions, buttons and small keys, as well as difficulty in reading and writing extensive texts. Also their small screens, little memory, their limited power supply, and lower processing speed are a problem. If the limitations of the device are exceeded, pages are viewed incomplete.

13.7 Usability Evaluation Systems for Mobile Devices

Studies on usability interfaces for mobile devices are fairly recent [11]. The W3C established a working group (Best Practices Working Group [5]—or BPWG) to study these issues and develop guidelines to follow when designing websites for mobile devices.

Through the BPWG, the first outline of recommendations for developing websites for mobile devices was introduced and it is known as mobileOK [16]. MobileOK checks the suitability of mobile content as defined in W3C mobileOK Basic Tests 1.0, which is based on W3C Mobile Web Best Practices 1.0. Both documents are still in working draft and recommendation proposal respectively.

13.7.1 Basic Tests of MobileOK

As the W3C document explains, the outline defines mobileOK requirements, and how they can be detected and evaluated. Its foundation is the best practices document for mobile web.

The mobileOK scheme is divided into two levels: the first level "represents a first step towards creating an effective user experience for mobile users," as stated in the document, while the second level is "a substantially larger step towards that end."

It should be noted that mobileOK is aimed at developers of content, tools, content providers, content discovery services (search engines), end users, and certification suppliers (validators).

There are several points which are evaluated when a webpage must be accessible via mobile phone, of which we emphasize:

- The mime type must match any of the following: application / vnd.wap.xhtml + xml or application / xhtml + wml.
- Avoid using absolute values in the style measures such as "px," "pt", etc.
- All images must include the attribute <Alt>.
- You can not include labels script, <object> or <applet> (as it has been explained before, several devices do not support them).
- The size of the document including style sheets should occupy less than 20 KB due to current bandwidth limitations.
- The document should include a title.

There are certain tools that automatically evaluate some of these aspects, including W3C Mobile Web Best Practices checker [15], a validation tool for mobiles (cell phones). However, there are important issues for mobile usability that can not be automated and require an expert for evaluation.

The Mobile WebA tools take into account this fact, combining the automatic evaluation with the necessary participation of experts in the evaluation process.

13.8 Evaluation of Accessibility for Mobile Devices

As already mentioned, accessibility is the set of characteristics which should provide an environment, product, or service to be usable in terms of comfort, security, and equality for all people, particularly those with disabilities.

There are various applications and/or devices which help users handle problems with a website interface. One of them are talks [16], which adds to Symbian operating system mobile devices the ability to read what is presented on the screen. Another one is Mobile Speak Pocket [4], a full-screen reader for Pocket PC devices.

But for these tools to be able to assist and fulfill their function, the design [20] and website creation needs to follow accessibility guidelines, such as introducing alternative texts to add multimedia elements [6].

Associating accessibility guidelines to those of Website Content Guidelines (WCAG 1.0) developed by the World Wide Consortium, each pattern has one or more verification points that help detect possible errors.

13.9 Best Practices in Mobile Web 1.0

The W3C [18], with the aim of making access to the Web from a mobile device into something as simple and convenient as it is from desktops, has launched the initiative "W3C Mobile Web Initiative" [17]. It seeks to solve the problems of interoperability and usability that currently impede access to the Web from mobile devices and enable one of the main objectives that the W3C is trying to achieve, one Web for all. It would transform the Web into a platform for ubiquitous services completely transparent to the user.

The W3C announced the move to candidate for recommendation of Good Practices in Mobile Web 1.0. [5]. Prepared for website designers and content managers, these guidelines describe how to create Web content that works properly on mobile devices. There are at least 60 guidelines to be followed to create pages accessible and usable from mobile devices.

13.10 Group of Apllications WebA mobile

The Mobile Web tools, currently under development, will consist of a suite of applications or tools to assist in designing and evaluating websites.

13.10.1 Evaluation Package

The evaluation package contains the procedures involved for assessing the usability and accessibility of user interfaces. This combines different methods of evaluation: automatic, heuristic, based on standards and/or rules.

The assessment of the usability of a website is somewhat complex and not all aspects can be validated automatically, although there are programs (such as Morae [7], Noldus Observer [9], or HTML Validator [14]) that assist in the process, some points can only be validated and verified by professional experts in usability. That is why WebA has been designed to be a tool where these experts share and check all their evaluations.

The heuristic evaluation [8] is based on the performance of a group of evaluators who follow a set of heuristic rules to discuss user interfaces (in this case interfaces in mobile devices) and determine their conformity or not based on established principles. This evaluation method is able to detect many of the issues of usability, but it is very expensive and time-consuming.

The evaluation based on standards and/or patterns consists in evaluating each point of the standards and/or patterns, by a team of experts. Each expert conducts a thorough inspection of the interface checking compliance, or otherwise, of each of the points identified in the standard.

Mobile WebA integrates both types of evaluation along with the guideline and/or standard based, for evaluating all aspects reducing the high cost in time and money from the heuristic evaluation. This evaluation package has several modules: verification module of ISO standards, verification module for Best Practices in Mobile Web 1.0, and evaluation module through user satisfaction tests.

13.10.2 Verification Module of ISO Standards

This module needs a main evaluator, responsible for determining the team members, working methods, managing and analyzing the results of each member. As a result, a report is then produced.

The standards are public documents containing technical specifications to be used voluntarily, based on results from experience and technological development. They are accepted by consensus of interested parties.

Its application in the evaluation process is to track each item that is specified in the standard, thus ensuring that we have reviewed every aspect mentioned in it.

The rules that apply directly to the development of user interfaces for mobile devices are the ISO / IEC 18201 (User interface for mobile devices. This standard contains specifications on the user interface for PDA's with the capability to exchange data with servers) and ISO 18789 (Ergonomic requirements and metric systems for screens. Standard which aims to revise and replace the ISO 9241 Parts 3, 7 and 8, and ISO 13406).

Mobile WebA will consist of modules based on semi-automatic verification standards and the recommendations cited.

13.10.2.1 Verification Module for Best Practices in Mobile Web 1.0 (W3C)

Before the W3C announced the move to *Candidate for Recommendation of Best Practices in Mobile Web 1.0.* [5], the Laboratory was already studying and working with the standards for the design of the WebA Mobile tools.

These patterns serve website designers and content managers in the creation of content that works properly on mobile devices. Mobile WebA verifies the fulfillment of these guidelines to evaluate the accessibility and usability of websites.

Among the 60 guidelines, we will discuss the most relevant which will be applied to the evaluation process: consistency of content, perform tests in actual devices as well as emulators, provide consistent navigation mechanisms, assign hotkeys to the navigation menu and functionality to those that are used most frequently (it is needed to analyze the logs and/or a user test), do not use image maps unless you know that the device supports them effectively, avoid pop ups, content suitable for the context of mobile devices, use a clear and simple language, limiting the scroll in one direction, do not use large images, avoid using frames, avoid using tables for page layout, use stylesheets, using concise and efficient code, do not rely that cookies are available, provide cache information on HTTP responses, and create logical order tabulation between elements of the website.

13.10.2.2 Evaluation Module Through User Satisfaction Test

Through this test the evaluator gains knowledge on what the user thinks about the structure, content, navigation, etc. of a website which in turn helps in the final evaluation of a site. This test is carried out after a user test, where a group of people use the site trying to find the solution to some questions that several experts have suggested (find a telephone number, send a complaint, buy something, etc.).

In the Aragonese Usability Lab these types of sessions are performed in an evaluation room and are video recorded. The session is monitored through the observation room. The group of evaluators can use the recordings to value or discern the test by users.

13.11 User Management Package

Mobile WebA has four types of users (Fig. 13.1): administrator, moderator, evaluator, and user who enters and completes the satisfaction test.

13.12 Session Evaluation Management Package

Mobile WebA allows for the generation of reports showing the results of accessibility standards and patterns [12]. It can also generate charts of the results from the evaluations based on standards. Mobile WebA provides a forum for communication of evaluator and moderators, for a better evaluation of the website.

13.13 Evaluation Process of a Site with Mobile WebA

Mobile WebA will follow a process of evaluating websites that is very similar to that of WebA [19]. This way it will cut the time of learning the new tool by experts on

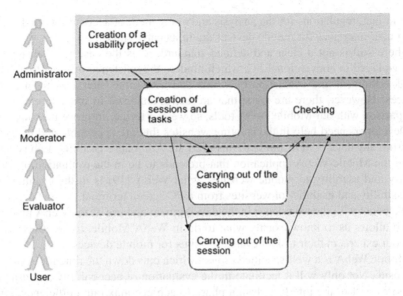

Fig. 13.1 Type of users and the relationships among them

Web accessibility and usability that are collaborating with the Aragonese Usability Lab in the evaluation of websites and that already know and work with WebA.

The process of evaluating a website is based on the participation of a group of experts who first worked on an individual basis with Mobile WebA, and then share their assessment to produce a single final report, result of the evaluation of user interface for mobile devices conducted by the Mobile WebA tools.

Once a session is created to evaluate a website by the Administrator and Moderator (applying the methodology and choosing the evaluators) the method of work for each evaluator will be the following: first, the website to be evaluated and the methodology to be applied are determined. Then, Mobile WebA verifies those points which it can automatically, and presents the results to the evaluator, allowing him/her to change any of the valuations that are deemed necessary. It follows a scale of 1 to 5, with 1 being the lowest possible case.

Mobile WebA stores data automatically and displays a report with the results to the evaluator, as required, including a link to the evaluated website.

13.14 Findings and Future Development

The need to access information from anywhere and from any mobile device is becoming ever greater. Furthermore, not all users have the same abilities nor all devices are equal. However, developers must think of everyone (users and devices) when designing a website to enable it to be accessible and usable. It is not an easy task; in fact, regulations for the analysis and assessment of accessibility and usability of user interfaces for mobile devices are in its early stages.

There still is not a clear and defined standard, as is the case for websites that are displayed in conventional PC, which hinders the existence of tools to assist in the development and evaluation of usable and accessible interfaces from mobile devices. However, there are some that are being analyzed in order to establish a comparison with our Mobile WebA tools, so we can further improve the tool.

Developers need help in the creating websites that are accessible and usable by all, from any device. In response to this need the Aragonese Usability Lab is developing the Mobile WebA application that pretends to be in the evaluation of accessibility and usability to mobile websites, what WebA [19] is in the evaluation of accessibility and usability of websites from a PC screen terminal.

We count with the experience in the development and use of the WebA platform, which allows us to know exactly what to do in WebA Mobile, to be effective and help our experts in their task of evaluating sites for mobile devices.

Mobile WebA is a well-specified project which cuts down the time for evaluating a website. Not only will it facilitate in the evaluation of accessibility and usability but will assist in the interface design phase to achieve maximum efficiency, effectiveness, and user satisfaction.

Mobile Web facilitates assessment of the usability by verifying the ISO/IEC 18021, ISO 18789, ensuring adjustment to these industry standards, and guidelines recommended by the W3C in its Best Practices in Mobile Web 1.0.

Mobile WebA will automate the evaluation of all those points that are possible, but without forgetting the necessary involvement of expert evaluators combining both modes of assessment.

It will also facilitate the necessary communication between experts who will, as it has already been proved with WebA, reduce the time and cost of meetings, and enable evaluators to consult and review previous revisions. It will also allow the automatic generation of the final report to adequately be presented to the client.

Acknowledgments This chapter has secured funding from the research project and multidisciplinary technological development "PM039/2006—usability, accessibility, and analysis of user satisfaction with the interface design applications for mobile devices" and "Aragonese Usability Lab" project of the Department of Science, Technology and University (Government of Aragon).

References

1. Alan D., Janet, F., Gregory, A., Russell, B. "Human–Computer Interaction". Prentice Hall, 2004
2. Laboratorio Aragonés de Usabilidad (http://www.laboratoriousabilidad.org).
3. Laboratorio Avanzado sobre Aplicaciones Jurídicas y Empresariales en la Sociedad de la Información (http://labje.unizar.es)
4. Mobile Speak Pocket de Codefactory. (http://www.codefactory.es/mobile˙speak˙pocket/ mspeak˙pocket.htm)
5. Mobile Web Best Practices 1.0 (http://www.w3.org/TR/2006/PR-mobile-bp-20061102/)

6. Mobile Web Developer's Guide. Part I: Creating Simple Mobile Sites for Common Handsets. 2007
7. Morae (http://www.morae.com).
8. Nielsen, J. & Molich, 1990. Heuristic evaluation of users interfaces.
9. Noldus Observer (http://www.noldus.com).
10. Parque Tecnológico Walqa (http://www.ptwalqa.com).
11. Paterno, Fabio (2003): Understanding interaction with mobile devices. In Interacting with Computers, volume 15. (http://www.elsevier.com, http://www.sciencedirect.com)
12. Pautas de Accesibilidad al Contenido en la Web 1.0 (http://www.discapnet.es/web_accesible/wcag10/WAI-WEBCONTENT-19990505_es.html
13. I Plan Nacional de Accesibilidad 2004-2012 (http://www.imsersomayores.csic.es/documentos/documentos/mtas-planaccesibilidad-01.pdf)
14. W3C MarkUp Validation Service (http://validator.w3.org/).
15. W3C Mobile Web Best Practices checker. Herramienta de validación para móviles. (http://validator.w3.org/mobile).
16. W3C mobileOK Basic Tests 1.0 (http://www.w3.org/TR/2007/WD-mobileOK-basic10-tests-20070130/)
17. W3C Mobile Web Initiative (http://www.w3.org/Mobile/)
18. W3C: World Wide Web Consortium (http://www.w3.org/)
19. WebA: Herramienta de ayuda para el diseño y evaluación de websites. Interacción 2006.
20. http://www.usabilitynet.org/tools/cardsorting.htm

Chapter 14
Requirement Gathering Templates for Groupware Applications

Victor M.R. Penichet, Maria D. Lozano, José A. Gallud,
and Ricardo Tesoriero

Abstract   This chapter presents a novel approach to gather requirements for groupware applications, i.e. an application designed to be used by several users through a net of computers such as the Internet. In this chapter we propose several extensions to traditional templates typically used to gather requirements in order to include those requirements specifically related to groupware applications that currently cannot be described with traditional templates. The methodology we propose may be integrated in a process model to identify the roles and tasks needed in the following stages of the development process starting from the new requirements specification.

14.1 Introduction

Groupware applications are becoming more and more usual every day. They are applications where users achieve common objectives by performing tasks through networks. They collaborate, cooperate, coordinate, and/or communicate with each other. Users are not considered as individual members but as members of groups which interact among them. Such applications have particular features that if they were taken into account explicitly from the beginning could improve the quality of the final system [4, 8–10, 13–15].

In this chapter we present a proposal to gather such particular features. Traditional techniques such as brainstorming or interviews may be used to collect the information. Then, templates are used to describe the information to be gathered [3]. Some specific metadata are proposed regarding the most important features concerning groupware applications.

We have applied this approach in a complete process model to collect the requirements of groupware applications in the first stage of the software life cycle:

V.M.R. Penichet (✉)
Computer Systems Department, University of Castilla-La Mancha 02071 Albacete Spain
e-mail: victor.penichet@uclm.es

J.A. Macías et al. (eds.), *New Trends on Human–Computer Interaction*,
DOI 10.1007/978-1-84882-352-5_14, © Springer-Verlag London Limited 2009

requirements gathering. This metadata is integrated in the whole process model. Moreover, the traceability among the different stages has been accurately defined. Requirements and actors are identified and described in the requirements gathering stage and they are used to identify tasks and roles in the analysis stage. It is an automated process which may even generate use case diagrams automatically. In this chapter we describe the metadata concerning groupware applications that we consider important to specify such particular software.

The rest of the chapter is structured as follows: Section 14.2 briefly shows the use of templates in the requirement gathering stage. The templates and the metadata we propose in the requirements gathering of groupware applications are described in Section 14.3 including some examples. Finally, some conclusions about the work are presented in Section 14.4.

14.2 Templates to Specify the Requirements

Some process models for Requirements Engineering provide three stages: requirements gathering, requirements analysis, and validation. We have based our proposal on the Amador Duran's process model [3], which matches with this three-stage approach and proposes some techniques in each one. In the first stage, he proposes some templates to gather information to specify a system. We extend these templates with some other metadata we consider important for the specification of groupware applications, as well as some new templates have been developed following the same purpose.

Known techniques for requirements gathering may be used in this stage to identify important data about the system:

- Interviews are a natural way of communication among people. Some authors [12] consider three steps: the preparation of the interview, the interview itself, and then the analysis of the results.
- The Joint Application Development (JAD), the IBM technique developed in 1977, usually provides good results; however it takes too much time and too many people.
- The brainstorming is widely used because it is very easy to implement and ideas are generated easily.
- Use Cases, which were proposed by Jacobson in 1993 [8], are traditionally used in Software Engineering especially in UML [1, 11] for specifying the required usages of a system.
- Observations, study of documentation, questionnaires, immersion, are some other common techniques.

The previous techniques or any other one may identify the information which is necessary to specify a system. Templates are a way to put such information in a semi-formal manner.

Durán proposes several steps to gather the requirements of a system. First you should collect the information regarding the problem domain in the current system or in the current context. Then system objectives are identified and described by means of specific templates. Such system objectives come from the division of the main problem in several sub-problems by following the *divide-and-conquer* technique. Once the main problem has been divided, functional requirements, non-functional requirements, and information requirements are identified in every system objective. Such requirements are also described by way of specific templates whose metadata specify every requirement. Finally, requirements and objectives are organized and prioritized. In the later sections the templates and the metadata we propose for groupware applications will be described.

As a result of this requirements gathering stage, Durán proposed a System Requirements Document. This document consists of a manuscript containing all the information which have been gathered and organized by means of the several templates. One of the key points are the traceability matrixes, which make explicit some information and relationships among requirements and objectives which is implicit in the specification in order to provide the developer with an easy view.

14.3 Templates and Metadata for Groupware Applications

Based on Durán templates [3], we have defined the ones we consider necessary in order to gather the requirements for a groupware application. There is a template to gather the information regarding objectives and requirements which consist of three parts: a general template with the common metadata concerning both objectives and requirements, then a specific extension with different metadata for system objectives and for requirements, and finally a CSCW extension with metadata regarding groupware issues in case it is necessary. Every system objective is specified by way of a Use Case Diagram. The most important use cases will be described by means of such templates for requirements.

Since the participants of a groupware application should be taken into account as members of groups interacting among them and they are the key point in such systems, it is very important to gather information about them from the beginning. Some templates are proposed to accomplish this situation. First the participants as part of something else are considered by means of the organizational structure template. Then every participant is specified by specific templates. They may be actors, groups, individuals, users, or agents.

The aforementioned templates will be described in the following sub-sections and the methodology to accomplish this requirement gathering will be described later.

14.3.1 General Template for System Objectives and Requirements

The general template for system objectives and requirements contains the common metadata which describes the sub-systems in which the system has been divided, the functional requirements, the non-functional requirements, and the information requirements:

- Unique identification is *OBJ-<id>*, *IR-<id>*, *FR-<id>*, or *NFR-<id>* depending on the element to be described.
- *Version* allows changes and a record of them.
- *Author* addresses who is the person that has gathered this piece of information.
- *Sources* provides the origin of the information.
- *Importance* indicates how important this objective or requirement is.
- *Urgency* shows if the development of this objective or requirement should be carried out immediately.
- *State* indicates the current level of development if necessary.
- *Stability* shows the necessity of future changes.
- *Comments* provide a place where to note something else which is relevant.
- *Related Objectives* and *Related Requirements* bring system objectives and requirements into relationship.

Previous metadata were proposed by Duràn. Other two metadata have been introduced to consider awareness and who are the participants in the system:

- *Awareness issues* provide a way to know who should be informed about what, how, etc. Awareness is becoming more and more important due to the number of participants in groupware applications, and due to the amount of data managed. Such issue should be taken into account from the beginning. A metadata in this template is a first step. It is necessary to consider what is important to whom, i.e. a description of the information itself, the way they should be aware of such information, i.e. web notifications, email, avatars, etc.; when they should know the piece of information, where, and why. This metadata could be allocated into the CSCW extension in the general template because it concerns with information, however we have decided to introduce it on the general template because sometimes this information may be required from objectives or requirements which are not typically collaborative.
- *Participants* is a metadata which depicts who or which are doing something in the system. The most important thing is to know what they are going to do in the groupware application.

14.3.2 Objective, Requirements, and CSCW Extensions

In this sub-section the specific extensions for objectives and requirements, as well as those regarding CSCW issues, will be described. Metadata regarding requirements are the traditional information that should be considered when gathering them (they have been introduced in the templates by Durán), whereas the CSCW ones are part of our proposal. All these metadata contribute to complete the general template for system objectives and requirements.

The specific metadata regarding *objectives* are three: a *description* about the objective, and *up-dependences* or *down-dependences* which describe the hierarchical relationships among the different system objectives. As mentioned before, a system objective represents a sub-problem in which the main problem has been divided.

Information requirements have also three metadata: a specific *description*, information concerning *specific data*, and a *temporal range*, i.e. past and present or only present.

Functional requirements consider traditional metadata such as *pre-condition*, *normal sequence*, *post-condition*, *exceptions*, *frequency*, *performance*, and *description*.

Non-functional requirements only consider a *description* as a particular metadata extension.

When an objective or a requirement regarding groupware application issues is described by means of the templates, it is also necessary to consider the special groupware applications' features. The metadata proposed as a new extension is the following:

- *CSCW description.* In addition to the previous general description in the general template, it is possible to complete the specification of the objective and/or the requirement considering another description only with CSCW information. Such explanation describes their collaborative nature.
- *Environment description.* The environment where the requirement will be carried out should also be well-known: rooms, equipment, resources, etc.
- *CSCW features.* Those concerning coordination, collaboration, cooperation, and/or communication.
- *Time/space features.* Groupware applications could be synchronous or asynchronous, i.e. in real time or not, and in the same place or in different places.
- *Demand level.* For example, a surgical procedure made in the distance through a groupware application must work in real time and without any delay because a human life could be at stake. However, some delays may be allowed in a chat application.

From the requirements identified in this requirement gathering stage, the analysis stage will be able to identify the different tasks to be performed in the system.

As an example of use, Table 14.1 shows the specification of a functional requirement called *document edition* by means of the metadata of the general template and the extensions introduced for to consider the specific features concerning CSCW systems. *Document edition* is a requirement of a bigger case study about a system which provides users with a mechanism to elaborate and review documents among several people considering groupware issues.

Table 14.1 Description of the functional requirement called *Document edition* with the proposed template

RF-8	Document Edition
Version	1 (04/06/2007)
Author	• Victor M. R. Penichet (Researcher)
Sources	• Textual description from meetings
Related objectives	• #OBJ-3: Synchronous elaboration of documents to be published
Related requirements	• #{RI-<*id*>, RF-<*id*>, RNF- <*id*>} (<*requirements_name*>)
Importance	Very High
Urgency	High
State	Specified; To be implemented
Stability	Could change, but currently stable
Awareness issues	The following actors should be aware of this requirement:
	• #G-1 (AUTHORS):
	– *What*: an actor is modifying part of the current document
	– *How*: current modification is showed graphically
	– *When*: in real-time
	– *Where*: in the same workspace, in the same window
	– *Why*: to know who is modifying what and not to interfere
	– *What*: an actor modified a document
	– *How*: a past modification is showed by e-mail
	– *When*: after saving the current version, asynchronously
	– *Where*: in the actor's intranet and by e-mail
	– *Why*: to know who modified the document and what part
Participants	Actors which collaborate:
	• #G-1 (AUTHORS)
Comments	None
Description	The system will behave as follows when a user belonging to the group #G-1 (AUTHORS) edits the document.
Pre-condition	The document exists; the user is a registered one belonging to the group #G-1 (AUTHORS); a work session has been started

Normal sequence	Step	Action
	1	The user select the document to be modified
	2	The use case RF-7 (Session validation) is performed
	3	The use case RF-9 (Document validation) is performed
	4	The user selects the tool to be used
	5	The user marks where the change will be done in the document
	6	The user makes the modifications
	7	The system notifies the modifications to the authors
	8	The user saves the modifications
	9	The system notifies the modifications by e-mail and in the intranet

Post-condition	Save or lose changes	
Exceptions	Step	Action
	–	–
Performance	Step	Time
	7	Real-time
	9	Asynchronously
Frequency	Several times in every session and in every user	
CSCW description	Because of the collaborative nature of the current requirement:	
	• Notifications are necessary for user awareness	

Table 14.1   (continued)

RF-8	Document Edition
	• Insertion, modification, and modification in a document are issues to be careful. Awareness in real time is important. Some actions such as deleting an image could be too fast for the rest of authors to be aware. They should be aware in some way. • Real-time feeling in the document elaboration is important but not vital.
Environment description	The environment will be: • --
Coordination	No
Cooperation	Yes. A document is ela borated in real-time by several authors. There are critical sections where a user cannot modify anything if another does: check in / check out.
Collaboration	No
Communication	No
Space	Different
Time	Synchronous when editing a document: authors are aware of modifications in real-time. Asynchronous: when a document is saved, changes are sent by e-mail.
Demand level	Not so high.

14.3.3   Templates for the Organizational Structure, Actors and Extensions for Groups

As mentioned before, application's users may be geographically distributed, working in a synchronous way, and so forth. In the specification of software systems, social structures and users' collaborations are taken more and more into consideration so that the analysis of cooperative concerns can be done in depth. The organizational structure of the participants in a collaborative system represents the distribution of its elements.

Participants of the system and the relations among them are described by means of two templates: a template for the organizational structure of the participants of the system, and a template for each participant. If the participant is a group, an extension is provided.

Participants or organizational items compose the organizational structure of the participants of an organization, that is, they compose the logical structure of the users that will use a collaborative application:

- An *actor* is one or several persons or another external system that interacts with the system. Actors directly interact within the collaborative system to accomplish individual tasks, but they can also interact with each other, through the system, to perform cooperative tasks. This is a key aspect in the difference between human–computer interaction and human–computer–human interaction (CSCW).

This concept was firstly introduced by the object-oriented software engineering paradigm [8]. Nowadays, UML 2.0 [11] also uses this approximation. However, as it was pointed by Constantine and Lockwood [2], the use that Jacobson made of this term could be confusing because actor seems to mean the same as role. Constantine indicates that, colloquially, 'actor' refers to the person playing a part, and 'role' refers to the part being played.

The approach we use is closer to Constantine's one, thus actor does not represent the roles played by humans, hardware and other external systems, but such humans, hardware and other external systems.

An actor is a general concept which can be concretized into a group or into an individual item. In the same way, an individual item could be concretized into a user or an agent (defined later).

- A *group* is a set of individual or collective actors which play roles. Such a set of actors needs to interact together and to collaborate with each other in order to achieve a common objective. Common objectives would not be reachable without such collaboration. Groups can also be defined as part of other groups, so the whole organization could be seen as the largest group. A group itself can play a role.
- An *individual item* is a unique actor which plays a role. In other words, it is not a set of actors, but just one.
- A *user* is a human individual item who interacts with the system. We understand that some other artifacts could also interact with the system, and these artefacts could not be people. Accordingly, an agent is a non-human individual item. All the users are actors. All the agents are actors. But neither all the actors are users, nor agents.

From the description of every participant in the system, the analysis stage will be able to identify the different roles to be played by the participants in the system.

The template to describe the organizational structure of the participants includes the following metadata:

- *Version*, *author*, *sources*, and *comments* metadata have the same meaning that the ones in the general template for requirements.
- Then *actors*, *groups*, *individual*, *users*, and *agents* are identified separately.
- Description outlines how the participants are organized, their hierarchical relationships, and other associations.

The template to describe the each participant includes the following metadata:

- *Version*, *author*, *sources*, and comments metadata have the same meaning that the ones in the general template for requirements.
- *Description* of the actor.
- *Supergroups* express belonging relationships between actors and groups and their relationships.

- *Up-hierarchy* and down-hierarchy depict the hierarchical relationships among actors. For example, a user could be the boss of another one.
- *Other associations* among actors.
- *Capacities*. A capacity is an ability or a responsibility associated to an actor, which allows him to play certain roles and to perform tasks. Actors have capacities. Roles could require an actor to have some capacities in order to play such a role.

If the actor to be described is finally a group, it is also necessary to use the following metadata:

- *Common objective*. From the definition of group: "a group is a set of individual or collective actors which play roles. Such a set of actors needs to interact together and collaborate with each other in order to achieve a common objective."
- *Membership*. Since a group is a set of individual or collective actors, membership outlines such relationship.
- *Laws*. A law is a rule required by a group. This law conditions which actors could belong to the group according to social rules, cultural rules, actor's capacities, etc.

14.4 Conclusions

In this chapter a proposal to the requirements gathering stage for groupware applications has been presented.

The approach extends the proposal of Amador Durán [3] who uses templates to gather the information at the very beginning after using traditional techniques such as brainstorming or interviews. We have modified, elaborated, and extended such templates with particular metadata regarding groupware applications.

The templates and the metadata we propose provides information about the system objectives, the information requirements, the non-functional requirements, the functional requirements, the organizational structure of the participants in a system, and the participants of the system. A participant may be identified as an actor, a group, or an individual item, i.e. a user or an agent.

This proposal has been used in a complete process model to collect the requirements of groupware applications in the first stage of the software life cycle: requirements gathering. This metadata was integrated in the whole process model. Requirements and actors are identified and described in the requirements gathering stage and they are used to identify tasks and roles in the analysis stage. It is an automated process which even may generate use case diagrams automatically.

In this chapter we describe the metadata concerning groupware applications that we consider important to specify such particular software.

Acknowledgments   This work has been partially supported by the grants JCCM PAI06-0093-8836 (Junta de Comunidades de Castilla-La Mancha) and TIN2008-06596-C02-01 (Ministerio de Ciencia e Innovación).

References

1. Booch, G., Rumbaugh, J., Jacobson, I.: The Unified Modeling Language User Guide. Addison–Wesley,1999
2. Constantine, L. L. and Lockwood, L. A. D.: Software for use: a practical guide to the models and methods of usage-centered design, Addison Wesley, Reading, Mass, 1999.
3. Durán, A.: Un Entorno Metodológico de Ingeniería de Requisitos para Sistemas de Información. Doctoral Thesis. University of Sevilla. 2000
4. Greenberg, S.: The 1988 conference on computer-supported cooperative work: Trip report. ACM SIGCHI Bulletin, 21(1), pp. 49–55, July 1989.
5. Greif, I.: Computer-Supported Cooperative Work: A Book of Readings. Morgan Kaufmann, San Mateo CA, 1988
6. Grudin, J. CSCW: History and Focus. University of California. IEEE Computer, 27, 5, 19–26. 1994
7. Horn, Daniel B., Finholt, Thomas A., Birnholtz, Jeremy P., Motwani, D., Jayaraman, S.: Six degrees of Jonathan Grudin: a social network analysis of the evolution and impact of CSCW research. ACM conference on Computer supported cooperative work, pp. 582–591, 2004
8. Jacobson, I.; Christerson, M.; Jonsson, P. y Övergaard, G.: Object–Oriented Software Engineering: A Use Case Driven Approach. Addison–Wesley, 4a Edition, 1993
9. Johansen, R. (1988): Groupware: Computer support for business teams. New York: The Free Press
10. Johnson-Lenz, P. and Johnson-Lenz, T.: Consider the Groupware: Design and Group Process Impacts on Communication in the Electronic Medium. In S. Hiltz and E. Kerr (ed.), New Jersey Institute of Technology, Newark, New Jersey, 1981.
11. Object Management Group. UML Superstructure Specification, v2.0; 2005
12. Piattini, M. G., Calvo-Manzano, J. A., Cervera, J., Fernández, L.: Análisis y Diseño Detallado de Aplicaciones Informáticas de Gestión. ra–ma, 1996
13. Poltrock, S. and Grudin, J. 1994. Computer Supported Cooperative Work and Groupware. In C. Plaisant (ed.) Conference Companion on Human Factors in Computing Systems (Boston, Massachusetts, United States, April 24-28, 1994), CHI '94, ACM Press, New York, NY, 355–356
14. Poltrock, S. and Grudin, J. 1999. CSCW, groupware and workflow: experiences, state of art, and future trends. In CHI '99 Extended Abstracts on Human Factors in Computing Systems (Pittsburgh, Pennsylvania, May 15-20, 1999). CHI '99. ACM Press, New York, NY, 120–121
15. Poltrock, S. and Grudin, J. 2005. Computer Supported Cooperative Work and Groupware (CSCW). In Interact 2005. Rome, Italy.

Chapter 15
Emotional Speech Synthesis in Spanish for Natural Interaction

Sandra Baldassarri, Eva Cerezo, and David Anaya

Abstract   New trends in Human–Computer Interaction (HCI) focus on the development of techniques that favor natural communication between users and machines. Within these techniques, natural language plays a basic and important role. However, for a good and natural communication, language is not enough: emotional aspects must be included in speech synthesis. This chapter describes a conversational interface that supports the communication between a user and a virtual character in real time, using natural and emotional language in Spanish. During the interaction with the user, the emotional state of the virtual character may change, depending on how the conversation develops. The emotions are expressed in the choice of different answers and in the modulation of the voice.

15.1 Introduction

The great development of information technologies has produced a growing interest in computer systems that do not require previous technological knowledge. Therefore, Human–Computer Interaction (HCI) techniques must be improved to provide a natural and personalized communication between users and machines.

One of the most used communication methods is natural language. Although this method has been extensively studied, relevant aspects still remain open. In order to obtain a more natural and trustworthy interaction, HCI systems must be capable of responding appropriately to the users with effective feedback [1]. Within verbal communication it implies to add variability in answers and the synthesis of emotions in speech [2]. This will facilitate the acceptance and credibility of the new generation of software and applications, especially if they have virtual characters as interfaces.

S. Baldassarri (✉)
Advanced Computer Graphics Group (GIGA), Computer Science Department, University of Zaragoza, Aragon Institute for Engineering Research (I3A), Spain
e-mail: sandra@unizar.es

J.A. Macías et al. (eds.), *New Trends on Human–Computer Interaction*,
DOI 10.1007/978-1-84882-352-5_15, © Springer-Verlag London Limited 2009

In this chapter we describe a system developed to allow the communication between a user and a virtual character in real time, by using natural language in Spanish. The system includes the recognition of emotions, so that the virtual human can choose the most adequate answer and modulates his/her voice depending on these emotions.

15.1.1 Related Works

The incorporation of emotion in voice is carried out by changes in the melodic and rhythmic structures [3]. In the last years, several works focus on the synthesis of voice considering the components that produce emotional speech. However, most of the studies in this area refer to the English language [4–6]. Considering the Spanish language, the work of Montero et al. [7] focus on the prosody analysis and modeling of a Spanish emotional speech database with four emotions. They make an interesting experiment on the relevance of voice quality in emotional state recognition scores. Iriondo et al. [8] present a set of rules that describes the behavior of the most significant parameters of speech related with emotional expression and validate the model using speech synthesis techniques. They simulate seven basic emotions. A similar study was made by Boula et al. [9], but getting the expressions of emotions of videos performed by professional actors in English, French, and Spanish.

Unlike most of the previous works, our system performs emotional voice synthesis in Spanish and it allows *interaction* and supports *real-time* communication with the user in natural language. Moreover, in this conversational interface the emotional state, which may vary depending on the relationship with the user along the conversation, is considered and expressed by the *modulation of the voice* and by *selecting the right answer for the user*. For this purpose, the system keeps information about the "history" of the conversation.

15.2 Overview of the Communication Process

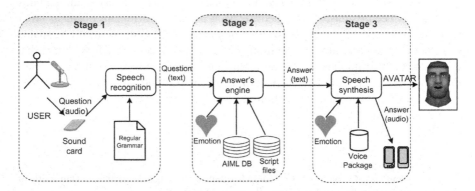

Fig. 15.1 Stages of the user-avatar voice communication process

The overall process of communication between user and avatar through voice is shown in Fig. 15.1. In the following sections, each of the three stages is explained.

Stage 1: Audio Speech Recognition (ASR)

The aim of this first stage is to obtain a text chain from the words said by the user in Spanish. To do this, a voice recognition engine has been constructed on the basis of Loquendo ASR (Audio Speech Recognition) software [10]. A recognition device based on a dynamic library of the ASR was created, and it enables

- to pick up the audio and prepare it for processing by the recognizer;
- to develop a grammar with the words that are going to be recognized;
- to process the results obtained from the recognizer function in order to know the recognized words (or noise);
- to establish the operation mode: synchronous or asynchronous.

Current recognizers use grammars to obtain an accurate response within a reasonable period of time. Loquendo ASR enables three possible context-free grammars, ABNF (Augmented BNF), XMLF (XML Form), and JSGF (Java Speech Grammar Format). Among these, we have chosen JSGF syntax as it avoids complex labeling of the XML and is used by a broader community than ABNF syntax.

One of the requisites of our system is that it must be able to "understand" and speak Spanish. This constraint prevented us from using existing open source libraries, all of them in English. Moreover, during the development of the recognizer, some problems that are specific to Spanish had to be solved: specifically, Loquendo ASR is not capable of distinguishing between words with or without 'h' (this letter is not pronounced in Spanish), with 'b' or 'v,' or with 'y' or 'll' (these letter pairs apply to one single phonemes). Neither is it useful when it comes to detecting the difference between words that are written in the same way but pronounced differently, where the difference is marked by an accent, for example the verb form "está" and the pronoun "ésta." We had to take all these factors into account when writing the words of the grammar and when creating the AIML categories (see Stage 2).

Stage 2: Getting the Right Answer

This stage is basically in charge of generating the answer to the user's questions in text mode (see Fig. 15.1). The system we have developed is based on chatbot technology under GNU GPL licenses: ALICE [11] and CyN [12]. However, CyN is only designed to hold conversations in English, so we had to modify the code to support dialogues in Spanish. The main differences lie in being able to work with accents, the "ñ" character, and opening interrogation and exclamation marks.

The search of the answers is based on a pattern recognition process: fixed answers are associated to patterns (static knowledge). These answers, however, vary depending on the virtual character's emotional state, or may undergo random variations so that the user does not get the impression of repetition if the conversation goes on for a long time (dynamic knowledge).

The knowledge of the virtual character is specified in AIML (Artificial Intelligence Markup Language) [13]. AIML is an XML derivative, which power lies in three basic aspects:

1. AIML syntax enables the semantic content of a question to be extracted easily so that the appropriate answer can be given quickly,
2. the use of labels to combine answers lends greater variety to the answers and increases the number of questions to which an answer can be given,
3. the use of recursion enables answers to be provided to inputs for which, in theory, there is no direct answer.

The AIML interpreter has been modified to include commands or calls to script files within the AIML category. These commands are executed when the category in which they are declared is activated and their result is returned as part of the answer to the user. This makes it possible, for example, to consult the system time, log on to a website to see what the weather is like, etc.

Stage 3: Text to Speech Conversion (TTS)

The voice synthesis is made using SAPI5 [14], a set of libraries and functions that enables to implement a voice synthesizer (in English), and, additionally, the Spanish voices offered by the Loquendo packages [10]. SAPI allows the obtaining of information about the visemes (visual phonemes) that take place pronouncing the phrase to be synthesized, what allows to solve the problem of lip synchronization. In order to avoid the voice to sound artificial, it has been equipped with an emotional component, as it is described in the following section.

15.3 Managing Emotions

15.3.1 Emotional State and Answers

In our system we work with the six universal emotion categories of Ekman [15]: joy, sadness, anger, surprise, disgust, and fear, plus the neutral one. Emotion is taken into account not only in the voice synthesis (as is explained in Section 15.3.2) but also in the generation of the answers, at two levels:

1. The answer depends on the avatar's emotional state. For this reason, the AIML < random > command has been redesigned to add this feature. Labels are used

for the different emotions (see Fig. 15.2). There may be more than one answer with the same label (in this case, one of these answers would be given at random) and there must always be an answer (applied to neutral emotional state) that does not have an associated label.

2. Besides, the emotional state of the virtual character may change during a conversation, depending on how the conversation develops. That is, if the conversation is on a topic that pleases the character, it gets happy; if it is given information it was not aware of, it is surprised; if it is insulted, it gets angry; if it is threatened, it gets frightened, etc.

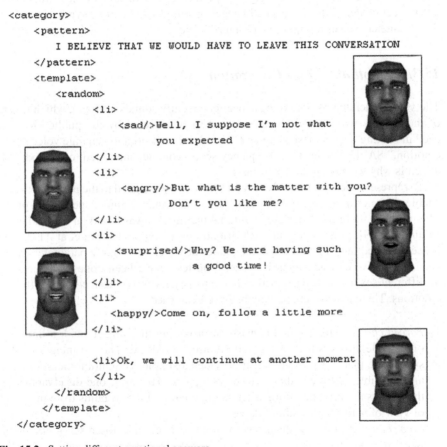

```
<category>
      <pattern>
            I BELIEVE THAT WE WOULD HAVE TO LEAVE THIS CONVERSATION
      </pattern>
      <template>
            <random>
                  <li>
                        <sad/>Well, I suppose I'm not what
                              you expected
                  </li>
                  <li>
                        <angry/>But what is the matter with you?
                              Don't you like me?
                  </li>
                  <li>
                        <surprised/>Why? We were having such
                              a good time!
                  </li>
                  <li>
                        <happy/>Come on, follow a little more
                  </li>

                  <li>Ok, we will continue at another moment
                  </li>
            </random>
      </template>
</category>
```

Fig. 15.2 Setting different emotional answers

Certain words in the user answers or questions are used to identify the user emotional state and to accordingly modify the virtual character emotional state. This is done through the execution of the appropriated script commands contained in the activated AIML category. The following category shows how when the user says an insult the virtual character gets angry:

```
<category>
 <pattern> YOU ARE SILLY </pattern>
 <template>
  <script>emotion=angry</script>
  I haven't insulted you
 </template>
</category>
```

After the execution of the "angry" script, the emotional state of the virtual character is set to angry: the sentence "I haven't insulted you" will be synthesized with the parameters corresponding to the "angry" voice.

15.3.2 Emotional Voice Generation

The voice generated by text-voice converters usually sounds artificial, which is one of the reasons why virtual characters tend to be rejected by the public. To succeed in making the synthesizer appear "alive," it is essential to generate voice "with emotion." SAPI5 enables tone, frequency scale, volume, and speed to be modified, which is why we have used it as a basis.

To represent each emotion, fixed values have to be assigned to the parameters that enable the relevant emotion to be evoked, in particular, volume, speed, and pitch. The initial configuration of these emotional parameters was based on the studies of Boula et al. [9], Francisco et al. [16], Iriondo et al. [8], and Barra et al. [17]. The process carried out to find the specific values at which these three parameters must be fixed was voice assessment by users. The tests have been done to 15 persons of different sex and age. They had to listen to sentences synthesized with different emotions. Three assessment paradigms have been used:

1. *Forced choice:* This method consists in providing the subjects with a finite set of possible answers that include all emotions modeled. The advantages of this system are that it is easy to use, it provides a simple recognition measurement, and it enables different studies to be compared. However, one disadvantage is that it does not provide information on the quality of the stimulus from the point of view of naturalness and lifelikeness.
2. *Free choice:* In this case the answer is not restricted to a closed set of emotions. Users mention the emotion they perceive, but without knowing which ones are modeled. This method is particularly suitable for finding unexpected phenomena during the experiment.
3. *Modified free choice:* In this case neutral texts (e.g., "my house is blue") are used together with emotion texts (e.g., "I can't believe it"). First of all, the neutral sentence is synthesized with the emotion prosody. The subject has to determine the emotion perceived. Then, the emotion text is synthesized. The result is taken

into account only if the correct emotion is detected in both cases. This way, a measurement of the impact of prosody in perception is obtained.

4. Once all the tests are made, the values of the parameters that control the emotional synthesis are adjusted and corrected, and assessment tests are made again. This process is repeated till the results are acceptable. The best perceptions are always obtained for sadness, anger, and disgust. The values of the emotional parameters validated by the tests are shown in Table 15.1.

Table 15.1 Setting volume, speed, and tome parameters for emotional voice generation

Emotion	Volume (0–100)	Speed (−10–10)	Pitch (−10–10)
Joy	80	3	4
Disgust	50	3	−6
Anger	70	3	0
Fear	56	1	2
Neutral	50	0	0
Surprise	56	0	3
Sadness	44	−2	2

15.4 Results

15.4.1 Basic Conversation with Virtual Characters

The system developed makes it possible for the user to maintain a conversation in Spanish with a virtual character. It has been added to a more general system, Maxine, that allows the real-time management of virtual characters and that is now being used in varied applications [18].

In particular, the dialogue system is being used to an application, MaxinePPT that generates, from powerpoint slides, 3D presentations performed by a virtual character. The new system allows natural language interaction (in Spanish) between the user and the virtual presenter: the user can ask questions about the presentation and get answers from the character. In fact, it is being used to improve the presentation of certain Computer Graphics issues in the Computer Science degree [19]. Also, the system is prepared to receive commands, functionality that has been developed in other application where a virtual character helps the user in the management of domotic system [20] (see Fig. 15.3).

15.4.2 System Performance

As far as the voice interface is concerned, we have endeavored to reduce to a minimum the time that elapses between the point at which the user finishes speaking and

Fig. 15.3 A user talking with a virtual character acting as a domotic assistant

the point at which the answer begins. Excessive lead time decreases the sensation of interactivity with the system and would not be readily accepted by the user.

The times corresponding to each stage in the communication process have been measured with sentences that are liable to be used during a conversation, in which the longest sentence is no longer than 20 words. The voice recognition and synthesis tests were carried out in Spanish. The time measurements in the search for results were carried out with Alice's brain [11], which has about 47,000 categories.

Table 15.2 shows a time study carried out through several conversations (with 20 users). In the table, the maximum time applies always to the recognition or synthesis of the longest sentences. Evidently, the longer the sentence, the longer it takes to process, but the synthesis times are always small compared to the recognizing times. The time difference between recognizing a one-word sentence and a twenty-word one is only of 0.41 seconds. This indicates that about 1.4 seconds are spent in the preliminary steps before recognition, which are independent of the length of the sentence.

In general, searching times are good, and the maximum time corresponds not to the longest sentence, but to the one that activates more recursive AIML operations.

Table 15.2 Time measurements of the different stages of a conversation in seconds

Stages of a conversation	Min. time	Max. time	Average
Speech recognition	1.6	2.01	1.78
Text to Speech	0.18	0.2	0.3
Search of Answers	0.1	0.17	0.2

Globally, times are acceptable as, in average, the duration of all three stages is about 2.28 seconds; this enables to establish a reasonable conversation rhythm suitable for real-time interaction.

15.5 Conclusions and Future Work

This chapter shows a voice dialogue system that enables natural and emotional interaction between a virtual character and the user.

The system works in Spanish and can be used to make enquires, to issue orders, or to just talk to a virtual character. The system understands the requests from the user and generates a suitable answer. This answer can be treated by another module of the application involved, or can be given back to the user directly, generated by voice synthesis.

To enable affective or emotional interaction, the character has an "emotional voice." The modulation of this emotional voice is accomplished by adjusting voice parameters such as volume, speed, and pitch. Moreover, the virtual character has been equipped with an emotional state that can be modified throughout the conversation with the user, depending on the user attitude or on the subject of the conversation. The answers offered by the virtual character may also vary depending on this emotional state.

The system is being successfully used in varied applications where virtual characters act in different ways: as virtual presenters, as educational tutors, or as assistants in domotic environments.

Related to future work, we are interested in improving the dynamic knowledge of the system in order to enrich the kind of conversations that can be carried out. Till now, just the "history" of the voice interaction is stored. In this way, we pretend to equip this conversational interface with a certain capacity of learning and reasoning or deduction [21]. Also, a more detailed evaluation of the impact of the emotional virtual characters and their acceptance by the users is still necessary [22].

Acknowledgments This work has been partly financed by the Spanish government through the TIN2007-63025 project and by the Aragon regional government through the Walqa agreement (Ref. 2004/04/86) and the CTPP02/2006 project.

References

1. Pantic M., Rothktantz L. "Toward an Affect-Sensitive Multimodal Human-Computer Interaction", Proceedings of the IEEE, Vol. 91 (9), pp. 1370–1390, 2003.
2. Cowie R., Douglas-Cowie E., Shroder M.: ICSA Workshop on Speech and Emotion: a Conceptual Framework for Research. Belfast, 2000
3. Bolinger D. "Intonation and its uses, melody and grammar in discourse", London: Edward Arnold, 1989.
4. Murray I., Arnott J. "Toward the Simulation of Emotion in Synthetic Speech: A Review of the Literature on Human Vocal Emotion", Journal of the Acoustical Society of America, Vol. 93 (2), pp. 1097–1108, 1993.
5. Shroder M. "Emotional Speech Synthesis: A review", Proceedings of the 7th European Conference on Speech Communication and Technology, Vol. 1, pp. 561–564, 2001.
6. Hoult C., "Emotion in Speech Synthesis", 2004
7. Montero J.M, Gutierrez-Arriola J., Colas J., Enriquez E., Pardo J.M, "Analysis and modelling of emotional speech in Spanish", Proceedings of the 14th International Conference on Phonetic, pp. 957–960, 1999.

8. Iriondo I., Guaus R., Rodriguez A., Lázaro P., Montoya N., Blanco J. M., Bernadas D., Oliver J. M., Tena D., Longth L. "Validation of an acoustical modelling of emotional expression in Spanish using speech synthesis techniques". Proc.ISCA 2000, pp.161–166.
9. Boula de Mareuil P., Celerier P., Toen J. Elan. "Generation of Emotions by a Morphing Technique in English, French and Spanish", Proc. Speech Prosody 2002, pp. 187–190.
10. Loquendo, http://www.loquendo.com/
11. Artificial Intelligence Foundation, http://www.alicebot.org/
12. Proyect CyN, http://www.daxtron.com/cyn.htm
13. Artificial Intelligence Markup Language (AIML) Version 1.0.1, http://www.alicebot.org/TR/2001/WD-aiml/
14. Microsoft Speech API 5.1 (SAPI5) http://www.microsoft.com/speech/default.mspx
15. Ekman P. "Facial Expression, The Handbook of Cognition and Emotion" John Wiley and Sons, 1999
16. Francisco V., Gervás P., Hervás R. "Expression of emotions in the synthesis of voice incontexts narrative". Proc. UCAmI2005, pp. 353–360, 2005.
17. Barra R., Montero J.M., Macías-Guarasa J., D'Haro L.F., San-Segundo R., Córdoba R. "Prosodic and segmental rubrics in emotion identification", Proc. ICASSP 2006 IEEE International Conference on Acoustics, Speech and Signal Processing.
18. Baldassarri S., Cerezo E., Serón F.J. "Maxine: a platform for embodied animated agents", Computers & Graphics (in press, doi: 10.1016/j.cag.2008.04.006), 2008
19. Seron F.J., Cerezo E., Baldassarri S. "Computer Graphics: Problem based learning and Interactive Embodied Pedagogical Agents", Proc. Eurographics 2008. Annex educational papers, pp. 173–180, issn 1017–4656, 2008.
20. Cerezo E., Baldassarri S., Cuartero E., Serón F., Montoro G., Haya P., Alamán X: "Agentes virtuales 3D para el control de entornos inteligentes domóticos", XIII Congreso Internacional de Interacción Persona-Ordenador, pp. 363–372, 2007 (in Spanish).
21. Kasap Z., Magnenat-Thalmann N. "Intelligent virtual humans with autonomy and personality: State-of-the-art", Intelligent Decision Technologies, Vol 1, pp. 3–15, 2007.
22. Ruttkay Z., Doorman C., Noot H. "Evaluating ECAs – What and how?", Proc. of the AAMAS02 Workshop on 'Embodied conversational agents – let's specify and evaluate them!', Bologna, Italy, July 2002.

Index